# Seven Schools of Macroeconomic Thought

# Seven Schools of Macroeconomic Thought

*The Arne Ryde Memorial Lectures*

Edmund S. Phelps

CLARENDON PRESS · OXFORD
1990

Oxford University Press, Walton Street, Oxford OX2 6DP
Oxford New York Toronto
Delhi Bombay Calcutta Madras Karachi
Petaling Jaya Singapore Hong Kong Tokyo
Nairobi Dar es Salaam Cape Town
Melbourne Auckland
and associated companies in
Berlin Ibadan

Oxford is a trade mark of Oxford University Press

Published in the United States
by Oxford University Press, New York

British Library Cataloguing in Publication Data
Phelps, Edmund S. (Edmund Strother)
Seven schools of macroeconomic thought — (The Arne Ryde
lectures).
1. Macroeconomics. Theories.
I. Title  II. Series
339.301
ISBN 0–19–828333–4

Library of Congress Cataloging-in-Publication Data
Phelps, Edmund S.
Seven schools of macroeconomic thought: the Arne Ryde lectures /
Edmund S. Phelps.
Includes bibliographical references.
1. Macroeconomics. I. Title II. Title: 7 schools of
macroeconomic thought. III. Title: Arne Ryde lectures.
HB172.5.P458 1990 339–dc20 89–49214
ISBN 0–19–828333–4

Typeset by Hope Services (Abingdon) Ltd.
Printed in Great Britain by
Biddles Ltd.,
Guildford and King's Lynn

ARNE RYDE
8 December 1944–1 April 1968

# The Arne Ryde Foundation

ARNE RYDE was an exceptionally promising young student on the doctorate programme at the Department of Economics at the University of Lund. He died after an automobile accident in 1968 when only twenty-three years old. In his memory his parents Valborg Ryde and pharmacist Sven Ryde established the Arne Ryde Foundation for the advancement of research at our department. We are most grateful to them. The Foundation has made possible important activities to which our ordinary resources are not applicable.

In agreement with Valborg and Sven Ryde, we have decided to use the funds made available by the Foundation to finance major arrangements. We have from 1973 arranged a series of symposia in various fields of theoretical and applied economics. In May 1988 at Snogeholm Castle in Skane Professor Edmund S. Phelps held some lectures entitled 'Recent Schools in Macroeconomic Theory', published here as the first issue in a series of Arne Ryde Memorial Lectures. A new issue in the series is planned to appear about every second year. We are indeed glad that Professor Phelps agreed to come to Sweden to give the first Arne Ryde Memorial Lecture.

Bjorn Thalberg

# Preface

THIS small book is a version for publication of the Arne Ryde lectures given at Lund University in May 1988. They are the first in a series of lectures under the sponsorship of the Arne Ryde Foundation.

It has been an unusual venture for me in a number of ways. There was, first, its method of total immersion. Though not known for a love of oratory, I found myself talking about macroeconomic theory for eight or nine hours in the space of two days. Happily, the audience of advanced students and assorted scholars managed to remain engaged the whole time, and so did the speaker. This was a gratifying experience.

There was another departure. Until then I had always worked on my own ideas. But this enterprise used the studio system, built around the producer. The subject of these lectures was entirely the idea of Bjorn Thalberg, who as head of the Ryde Foundation instituted the new lecture series. He suggested to me that one could divide macroeconomics these days into a number of schools of thought and that there would be a wide audience for an appraisal of their progress and prospects. The work of defining the schools and evaluating them was left to me. This arrangement was conducive to more risk-taking, I suspect, than would have resulted had the whole responsibility for the enterprise rested on me.

The opportunity to share my views on present-day macro-economics seems to me to come at the right moment. Some observers consider macroeconomics to be in a sorry state, confused by recent experience and riven by methodological dissension. I agree it is destructive when the more zealous participants wage a crusade to exclude or demote other approaches and other questions. Some of the combatants, in the heat of battle, seem to see themselves in a Western epic between good guys and bad guys, a second Methodenstreit a century after the first.

To me, however, it is the most interesting time in macro-economics since the rise of micro-macro theory in the 1960s. It is a time in which macroeconomists are again entertaining new hypotheses about the mechanisms governing the economy and reaching out for a new 'paradigm'—not all reaching in the same direction, of course. To me the recent empirical puzzles and the increased diversity of approaches constitute another demonstration that no school can expect its approach to be right for every place and period. Pluralism is best, and recurrent outbreaks of pluralism are inevitable in any case.

I see seven living schools of thought to be of importance in macroeconomic theory today. These are all thriving schools with an active research programme, however numbered their days. Some once-important schools from which the profession has moved away have not made it to the grand list.

Friends have suggested that the thesis of exactly seven extant schools is an artifice of the imagination, like the seven pillars of wisdom or the seven kinds of ambiguity. I suspect they think that three or four macroeconomic schools would be quite enough.

The distinctions I have made were a function of the aspects of macroeconomic theory to which I have been particularly attracted. Much of my interest in macroeconomics has been directed to price-wage setting and to the role of expectations, and making distinctions among models with respect to those aspects leads easily to a larger number of schools than are commonly defined.

One dimension along which we can classify schools of thought pertains to the treatment of wages and prices. Some of the more recent models contain, explicitly or implicitly, either real-wage rigidity in some sense or real-wage stickiness. The contrasting asynchronicity models possess one or another kind of impediment to the adjustment of nominal wages or prices, which gives rise to a stickiness in the average wage or price level. (While in any day some wages may be changing, most wages or prices are temporarily unchanging because of threshold or scheduling effects.) Finally there is a great variety of models in which all prices and wages are simultaneously and unreservedly flexible at every moment or with every period: the island parable, with its notion of market clearing in each local auction market, is one example of this framework; but it need not make any fundamental difference if each firm has to post each period its own wage scale and price list.

The other dimension refers to expectations. In the framework that was common until the rise of rational expectations, the expectations of people are to a degree exogenous—partly a matter of their experience and their 'knowledge', and not therefore entirely a function of the current state of the economy and its current structure. This approach emphasizes the incomplete communication between the members of a social economy and the consequent problem of co-ordination. Another approach adopts the premiss of rational expectations.

The seven schools I discuss can easily be located in the above three-by-two classification. Encamped under the banners of non-rational expectations and wage-price flexibility are those following in the footsteps of Keynes—the true Keynesians. In the same camp, but with a quite different outlook in some other respects, are Friedman and the traditional Monetarists. The New Classical school differs in adopting rational expectations, while the New Keynesian school departs by using models generating stickiness in the money-wage or money-price level. Supply-side macroeconomics fits along the New Classicals, differing only in the roles it assigns to monetary and fiscal policy. The Neo-Neoclassical 'real' theory of fluctuations also exhibits price-wage flexibility and rational expectations, though it is non-monetary in character. Finally there is a group of recently arrived models invoking real-wage rigidity or stickiness, with or without rational expectations, which I have taken to calling the Structuralist school.

No school so radical as to posit both non-rational expectations and real-wage rigidity has yet sprung up, and the infant school of non-rational expectations and nominal wage-price stickiness is now dormant. Two of the combinations in the above classification scheme are therefore not represented—and two of the combinations are over-represented—so if our only interest were in the above two dimensions of macro models it would be enough to sample one school from the four represented. But which school to deny, Keynes or Friedman? I have met the problem by giving them each fewer pages than I would have, had either of them been the sole representative in its category.

Even this brief project has drawn upon quite a few others, some of whom I would like especially to acknowledge. Dennis Snower and Bjorn Thalberg read and commented upon the entire draft. Roman Frydman and Axel Leijonhufvud focused on the difficult Keynesian chapter. Phillip Cagan read the Monetarist essay and Ricardo Caballero read the New Keynesian essay. Robert Mundell commented upon the Supply-Side chapter, Jean-Paul Fitoussi the Structuralist chapter. They are not responsible, of course, for the remaining mistakes, of which there are surely many. I thank them for their contribution.

I am very grateful to Kumaraswamy Velupillai for the generous part he played in this project from the earliest stage through to publication.

Finally I thank Bjorn Thalberg for his reliable support.

# Contents

# 1

# The Macroeconomics of Keynes

THE Keynesian school I will be discussing is a living school of thought, with a research agenda that has never been more actively pursued than in the past decade. As the label I have given it serves to indicate, this school draws crucial inspiration from the theoretical outlook brought to macroeconomics by John Maynard Keynes. But, of course, every school that calls itself in some way Keynesian claims such an inspiration.

The particular Keynesian school discussed here sees Keynes as the founder of its central theme: that the process of individual learning and market adjustment in response to altered opinion about the uncertain future is capable of going awry in the environment of uncoordinated and imperfectly informed decision-making provided by market capitalism. This school is thus differentiated, at least in emphasis, from the neo-Keynesian, post-Keynesian, and New Keynesian schools.

Keynes left so challenging a task for his successors that it has still not been accomplished to everyone's (or perhaps anyone's) satisfaction. The members of his school still admit to occasional rereadings of the founding work—not as holy writ, needless to say, but as a source-book for perceptive observations and theoretical suggestions.[1] It is a sign of how rich a source this work is that, as my colleague Brendan O'Flaherty wrote, it 'has not yet been fully mined'. While this Keynesian school of thought is older than the others I will be discussing, then, I estimate it to be farther from being spent than most of the others, one or two of which may be almost played out.

The founding work, of course, was Keynes's 1936 book, *The General Theory of Employment, Interest and Money.* Here

Keynes tackled a very big question about market economies, the causes of wide swings in economic activity, particularly of long slumps. If one had to sum up in one sentence the thesis of this great book, with perhaps a minor amount of interpolation between the lines, it is the proposition that the valuation of assets is sometimes disturbed by a massive shift of business or financial opinion and, in response, the labour market is not generally able to adjust rapidly and dependably so as to maintain the normal volume of employment, not because of any slow-workingness in the wage-setting machinery—wages may be quite flexible—but because the participants in that market cannot assess every shift in business or financial opinion that occurs nor the scale of the wage adjustment that each such shift requires.

To produce a manageable analysis it was necessary to make some critical choices. The theory chosen by Keynes was

monetary in an important way, assigning a crucial role to the current level of nominal wages;

intertemporal and 'capitalistic', assigning a key place to fluctuations in the natural state of interest, or 'marginal efficiency of capital', as determined in a two-sector economy;

fundamentally anti-equilibrium (in the expectational sense of the term), invoking uncertainty as an obstacle preventing or impeding expectations from successfully co-ordinating business activity;

interventionist to a degree in depicting monetary and fiscal instruments as having the power to make a difference and, up to a point, improve the stability of the economy.

With a vision of the economy narrowed to this extent, Keynes still faced the challenge of making vast and deep extensions of 'general equilibrium' as Walras and, in their simpler models, Marshall and Fisher had left it.

In this chapter I want to focus on the latter two features of Keynes's approach—the role of uncertainty and Keynes's evolving view of optimal macroeconomic policy. Inevitably the roles of money and capital will find openings to slip into the discussion.

The driving force in Keynes's vision of the market economy was evidently in place fifteen years before the *General Theory* with the publication of *A Treatise on Probability* in 1921. The presumption that novel developments always are in store for a society in the future, as in the past, makes it impossible, Keynes suggested, to assign an objective probability distribution to future states. In fact, '[not] all probabilities are measurable' (Keynes 1921: 34) because it is not generally possible to enumerate all the possible states of the world. Hence expectations are, in part and to a degree, arbitrary.

The importance of this uncertainty over people's economic prospects was underlined in a much later discussion by Keynes.

By uncertain knowledge . . . I do not mean merely to distinguish what is known for certain and what is only probable. The game of roulette is not subject, in this sense, to uncertainty . . . Even the weather is only moderately uncertain. The sense in which I am using the term is that in which the prospect of a European war is uncertain, or the price of copper and the rate of interest twenty years hence, or the obsolescence of a new invention, or the position of private wealth owners in 1970. About these matters there is no scientific basis on which to form any calculable probability whatever. We simply don't know. (Keynes 1937: 213–14)

One of the roots of such uncertainty, I would comment, comes from the fact that society cannot have objective knowledge now of the knowledge and values that society will come to have only in the future, with discovery and learning. To have such knowledge would be to have knowledge of what we do not now know. In addition, even if there were not that difficulty, the fact is that many disturbances to the economy are not being drawn constantly from a stationary probability distribution— even the climate is evolving; nor are the economy's reactions stationary, since institutions and policies also evolve.

With the conception of the *General Theory* a corollary fell into place. In a social economy having a degree of individual enterprise, hence having a market sector, the probabilities that an individual actor intelligently assigns to states tomorrow— and to states today in so far as they cannot be observed today by the individual—must depend upon the individual's beliefs, or 'expectations', about the probabilities that the others in the economy are assigning to those same states. Although the adage that 'believing makes it so' is a very special case—everyone's sudden belief that the average wage has dropped 10 per cent will not by itself cause the actual average wage or anyone's wage actually to fall by 10 per cent—believing generally matters. (In a labour market of flexible wages, yet imperfect information, the actual average wage would fall by some amount if everyone suddenly thought the average wage had just dropped. In a product market with a delay from input to output, the actual price in the future would fall if expectations of the price prior to input decisions suddenly increased.) Knowing this, sophisticated actors forming their expectations will attempt to forecast not only the exogenous or predetermined factors bearing directly upon the wage or price to be predicted but also upon the expectations of the other actors whose behaviour will affect the wage or price. Keynes's oft-cited example of a rather peculiar newspaper contest (1936: 156) served to dramatize the role played by the individual participants' guesses about 'average opinion' in the stock market. Since there is at best only a 'flimsy' basis for estimating average opinion, it is a factor that compounds the uncertainty attaching to the stock market and to the state of the economy generally.

There is little doubt that Keynes was right about the stock market. A participant in financial markets would handicap himself if he tried to get along merely with superior information and analysis concerning the underlying objective factors at work—the so-called fundamentals. It is necessary to know the analyses of others in order to judge the extent to which the market has over-discounted or under-discounted a possible future disturbance. To the suggestion that an investor could rely on the law of averages to neutralize non-fundamentals, the Keynesian reply is that a poor return one year puts the investor behind schedule in his accumulation forever after; there is no presumption of a good return later that will offset the poor return (as if there were sampling without replacement).

This was radical stuff. In pressing on economists the uncertainty of future conditions, the difficulty of gauging the analyses of others, and the consequent impossibility of a collective mind and collective rationality, Keynes was the bearer in economics of the intellectual revolution of his time. His outlook paralleled what was turning up in much of art and philosophy—in the cubism of Picasso and Braque, the atonalism of Schoenberg and Berg, the fragmented poetry of Eliot and Pound, and various writings from Nietzsche to Sartre. Keynes brought to economics the outlook generally called modernism: the consciousness of the distance between self and others, the multiplicity of perspectives, the end of objective truth, the vertiginous sense of disorder.

This parallel has continued to a new chapter, for in economics as in some other fields there is now a post-modern inclination to retrenchment back toward classical values. Keynes himself evidently felt that some of his followers had gone too far when he complained of 'much modernist stuff, gone wrong and turned sour and silly' (Keynes 1946: 186). Macroeconomics has been the field for a see-saw struggle over the past decade between the modernists—the asymmetric information camp and the expectational disequilibrium crowd—on one side and on the other side the divers post-modernists: the classicals in modern dress who march under such banners as New Classical and neo-neoclassical. This present-day Methodenstreit is a large part of what motivates this critical survey.

The stock market was the staging ground, in Keynes's account, where disturbances arose to attack the economy. The macroeconomic trouble caused by this market lay in its instability. Keynes held the price level in this market to be unstable not in the sense of a high variance but rather in the sense that a small amount of bad news, perhaps coming on top of a previous accumulation of bad news, or simply a random weakening of share prices—the cause unknown—might precipitate a stock-market crash—a drop of prices out of all proportion to external events. The prevailing convention according to which shares are priced abruptly cracks.

It is not surprising that a convention, in an absolute view of things so arbitrary, should have its weak points. It is its precariousness which creates no small part of our contemporary problem of securing sufficient investment . . . A conventional valuation which is established as the outcome of the mass psychology of a large number of ignorant individuals is liable to change violently as the result of sudden fluctuations of opinion due to factors which do not really make much difference to the prospective yield, since there will be no strong roots to hold it steady . . . In abnormal times, the market will be subject to waves of optimistic and pessimistic sentiment. (Keynes 1936: 153–4)

Obviously we badly need a sequel to the General Theory that serves to formalize this valuable insight. But to complain that Keynes was obscure and, lacking a mathematical formulation, ought not to have bothered is to be unappreciative or ungrateful.

Some members of Keynes's school have managed to add a little to the portrait of speculative behaviour started by Keynes. In a survey paper on speculation (Phelps 1986) I noticed an apparent pattern in recent empirical observations and econometric findings, a pattern consistent with Keynes's view. At least in short sample periods, short enough to fall within the span of a single convention (or subjective model) for valuing assets, there is estimated to be an under-responsiveness to events. Long-term interest rates show insufficient weight given to information about current disturbances, according to an analysis by Mankiw and Summers (1984). Exchange rates likewise show a muted response to current events, according to studies by Wadhwani (1984) and by Goodhart (1987). Company forecasts of their own future production levels display an analogous tendency to underweight the news and overweight history, according to the study by Mors and Mayer (1985). The tendency to under-react to news is consistent, as far as I can see, with an accompanying tendency toward waves of buying or selling as one 'convention' gives way—and comes to be seen as giving way—to another.

A deficient reactiveness to events is what we would expect if participants form expectations of the expectations of others and do not generally impute to others a response of expectations as large as the response in their own expectations. When a disturbance causes a sharp fall in the fundamentalist forecast, or rational expectation of long-term bond prices at tomorrow's market opening, the individual participant will adjust his own expectation of bond prices tomorrow by a much smaller amount unless and until he has some corroboration that the others in the market expect the same drop that he has calculated; with everyone in the market reasoning this way, the price of bonds will under-respond at the opening bell to the news of the disturbance. True, under sterile laboratory conditions, evidence of the size of the opening drop would immediately signal that everyone in the market had made the same calculation, contrary to expectation, and the market price would then suffer an after-shock that bumps it down to the fundamentalist level. But under real conditions, it will be understood that there is some chance the opening fall of the price was in part or wholly due to random causes. Thus the adjustment process tends to be drawn out.

The algebra of the basic argument is pretty clear from a simple model involving the expectations of the expectations of others to be found in the Frydman–Phelps conference volume on expectations (Phelps 1983).[2] My attention has recently been called to a new paper that from the same starting-point develops a somewhat similar argument in detail (Pemberton 1988).

The remaining task of the General Theory was to spell out the propagation mechanism: in particular, to show how this sort of instability in the speculative valuation of capital assets would lead to episodes of below-average (and above-average) employment. As is familiar to even the most casual students of the theory, there were three steps in the argument. A decline of speculative confidence—a drop, calculated at the initial level of employment, in what Keynes dubbed the marginal efficiency of capital—implies that there would have to be an equal decline in the nominal rate of interest if the product market were to remain in equilibrium at the initial level of employment.

Second, if the condition for money-market equilibrium is to be satisfied, a decline of the interest rate, in increasing the amount of money demanded, must be accompanied by a fall of real income, barring an increase of the money supply, unless the disturbance is accommodated by a decrease of the nominal wage level (hence of costs and prices). Third, nominal wages do not initially drop by enough, if at all, to forestall the fall of employment because workers in establishing their reservation money wage rates do not forecast adequately the extent and generality of the weakening of the demand for labour; and they do not complete at all promptly the adjustment necessary to return to the former employment level for reasons that Keynes did not make explicit but which may be presumed to involve workers' difficulties in gauging the extent and duration of the speculative disturbances. So there is a protracted spell of reduced employment as a result of the marginal-efficiency disturbance.

To go further it is useful to have a more formal model. The usual model, of course, has been Hicks's enormously successful IS–LM apparatus, which managed to telegraph the conclusions drawn from Keynes's propagation mechanism. But in that rendering of Keynes's mental equations the real prices of shares and of capital goods were no longer explicit; at best they were implicit, since in the parlance of those times a high long-term interest rate was taken to be synonymous with a low share price and a low demand price for capital goods.

The following mechanical sort of model of Keynes's system follows a formulation by Blanchard (1981) that brings back share prices. In these equations, the variable $q$ can be interpreted as 'Tobin's $q$', hence as the ratio of the real shadow price, or real *worth*, of installed capital, to the real *marginal cost* of producing capital, the latter being a constant in the one-sector case. A somewhat more elaborate pair of equations could justify interpreting $q$ as 'Keynes's $q$', so to speak, hence as the real demand price for capital goods in a two-sector set-up exhibiting a rising (real) supply price of capital-goods output. On all this, see Tobin (1969), Leijonhufvud (1968), and LeRoy (1983).

One relationship between $q$ and aggregate employment, $N$, corresponds to the IS curve, or investment–saving relation, of Hicks's model. Here final output is taken to depend upon $N$ and the capital stock, $K$, according to a neoclassical production function, F. Subtracting depreciation $\delta K$, from output gives income, $Y$, which is a function f of $N$ and $K$. Consumption expenditure, $C$, is made to depend upon income according to the usual consumption function, and upon a shift parameter $\theta$. Investment expenditure, $I$, is an increasing function of $q$ once the latter is high enough to induce positive gross investment. Government expenditure, $G$, is taken to be exogenous.

$$F(N, K) = C(f(N, K); \theta) + I(q) + G, \; C'(Y)<1, I'(q)>0. \quad \text{(IS)}$$

This equation is represented in the $(N, q)$ plane of Fig. 1.1 by the generally upward-sloping curve labelled $q^S$. It gives the 'supply price' in terms of $q$ of the investment implied by a given $N$, that is, the value of $q$ needed to induce that level of investment and thus the associated level of employment.

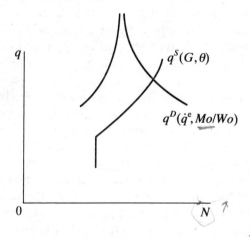

*Fig. 1.1.* IS-LM in the $(N, q)$ plane.

The other relationship between $q$ and $N$ corresponds to the Hicksian LM curve. It simply inverts the demand-for-real-cash-balances function to obtain wealth-owners' required money rate of interest, $i$, as a function, $\iota$, of income and real cash

balances; then it equates that to the expected nominal rate of
return on shares; the latter is the expected inflation rate, which
I will take to be a function of the level of employment and
which I will denote by $h(N)$, plus the expected real rate of
return on shares, expressed in terms of $q$ and its expected rate
of change as shown in the first term on the right-hand side.[3]
Letting $M$ denote the money supply, $W$ the money wage level,
and taking the price level to be marginal cost, hence equal to
$W/F_N(K,N)$, where $F_N$ is the marginal product of labour, we
have

$$\iota\{F(K,N),\ M_o/[W_o/F_N(K,N)]\} = (1/q)[F_K(K,N) - \delta + \dot{q}^e] + h(N),\ \iota_1 F_N + \iota_2(M/W)F_{NN} > (1/q)F_{KN} + h'. \tag{LM}$$

This equation is represented in Fig. 1.1 by the curve labelled
$q^D$. The inequality condition above stipulates that the required
interest rate rises with employment faster than the actual
nominal rate of return, other things being equal. Under this
condition, the LM equation must make $q^D$ decreasing in $N$ over
that range where $N$ is sufficiently large to cause $F_K - \delta + \dot{q}^e > 0$
and thus imply a positive expected real rate of interest. The
opposite is true where $N$ is so low as to make the expected real
rate negative.

I will confine attention here to the case in which only this
downward-sloping branch of the $q^D$ curve intersects the $q^S$
curve, at least over the range of parameter variation to be
considered. So I am working with instances of a unique
intersection of the two curves, which Fig. 1.1 illustrates.

This simplistic structure makes some useful points. Shocks
and shifts in opinion that induce changes in expectations of the
future, particularly in the expected rate of change of $q$, can be
said to operate through $\dot{q}^e$ to codetermine the resulting effects
on the levels of $N$ and $q$. A drop in the expected rate of change
of $q$ causes the current level of $q$ to drop and thus pulls $N$ down
alongside it.[4] No wonder then that the stock market is most
bullish at times when, as in October 1987, stocks are already
priced high by historical standards. One could as well say about
this system, however, that changes in expectations of the future

induce a change in the level of $q$ and thus (via IS) the level of $N$, and with the equations we can calculate the implied change in the expected rate of change of $q$. The diagram, like the original IS–LM diagram, has the shortcoming that it does not provide a complete dynamic analysis. It provides only a locus of eligible points $(q^e, q)$ from which, with luck, a full analysis will pick one. Of course, the rational-expectations approach, which is to calculate the model's correct-expectations path, as if everyone assigned the same probability to each possible event because these probabilities were objectively known and familiar to all, is studiously avoided by the Keynesian school.

To close the system it is necessary that the model should encompass the money wage rather than leaving it as an arbitrary parameter, as Keynes well understood from page 1 onwards. Not only did Keynes recognize that high and steady unemployment might well give rise to recurring wage cuts; he also took the current money wage level to be an increasing function of the current level of employment.

The contention that the unemployment that characterises a depression is due to a refusal by labour to accept a reduction of money wages is not clearly supported by the facts . . . [I]n the case of the general level of wages, it will be found, I think, that . . . [w]hen money wages are rising . . . real wages are falling; and when money wages are falling, real wages are rising. This is because, in the short period, falling money wages and rising real wages are each, for independent reasons, likely to accompany decreasing employment[,] labour being readier to accept wage cuts when employment is falling, yet real wages inevitably rising in the same circumstances on account of the increasing marginal return . . . when output is diminished. (Keynes 1936: 9–10.)

In my lexicon, the labour market described by Keynes exhibits flexible wages, though the firms have to set their own pay scales—there is no local auctioneer, let alone a global one—and there is little reason to imagine, however convenient it might be, that wages are reset continuously. We might just as well go along with present-day econometric habits by supposing that wages are subject to periodic review and that all wages in the economy are set afresh at the start of each such period, perhaps a quarter-year or half-year in length. There is more style than substance in supposing that the firms set the wage, however, since here, to be faithful to Keynes (and the island parable), I will assume that the firm offers only the wage it has to pay to attract the size of work force it expects it will need in the upcoming period; there is no rent to the worker such as arises in the incentive-wage models.

Keynes supposes that the amount of labour supplied to the market economy is a function not only of the average level of the real wage, in general, but also a function of the average level of the money wage—hence a function, given the real wage, of the general level of money prices. A drop of the money-price and money-wage levels would contract the amount of labour supplied at a stipulated level of the real wage. Keynes was somewhat fuzzy at places about the explanation of this non-classical influence. In his classic 1947 paper, James Tobin wrings his hands over the 'money illusion' that Keynes seemed to impute to workers and suggests a number of defences: (1) a union leadership is accountable for the relative wage it delivers, (2) the wage-earners have obligations fixed in terms of money, (3) workers have inelastic expectations with respect to the price level (which the money interest rate does not reflect), and (4) workers ignorantly mistake a reduced nominal wage for a reduced real wage, and some accordingly retire from the market. The last will be recognized as the somewhat strange model in Milton Friedman's celebrated 1968 paper on Phillips curves. Other writers saw in money illusion a Veblenesque effect of 'keeping up with the Joneses', as we say in my country. The theoretical and empirical adequacy of these defences remained under dispute in the ensuing years.

The seminal discussion of an imperfectly communicating market by Armen Alchian in 1970 and the idea of the 'island parable' in my 1969 preview of the 'new microeconomics' of employment theory (and in the introduction to the 1970 conference volume itself) led to the reinterpretation of Keynes's vision as one in which the worker is uninformed or poorly informed about the distribution of wage rates that would be available to him if he sought work in another community or trade. In this reinterpretation, a decline of jobs at a firm will occasion little reduction of the money wage because the workers do not suppose there to have been similar wage reductions elsewhere in the economy; it is a cut of the real wage rate relative to what is expected to be available elsewhere that meets a certain amount of 'resistance' because the affected workers assume they have these alternative opportunities. The supply of labour is a function of the real wage and the expected real wage elsewhere.

It will facilitate subsequent discussion to recall a few concepts connected with this informational model of the labour market. Call a state of affairs in which expectations are correct in some sense an 'equilibrium'. There exists, on weak conditions, a normal, or steady-state labour-market equilibrium character-ized by a normal volume of frictional unemployment that is the result of the vibrations, so to speak, going on all the time as some firms fail and new ones are born, and as workers aiming to see the world restlessly circulate between east and west, north and south. Hence in this steady-state equilibrium the average wage exceeds the wage (or average wage) that would be necessary to coax the corresponding volume of employment from the labour force if an all-seeing classical economist were brought in as a labour tsar to establish the least-cost allocation. Then there is a symmetry around this equilibrium. A fall of the wage relative to expectations—nominal or real, it is the same—induces a rise of unemployment, hence a fall of *em*ployment if the underlying disturbance is a drop in the demand for labour (not a rise in the supply); and, equally, a rise of the wages relative to expectations induces a fall of unemployment, hence a rise of employment if the disturbance is a rise of labour demand. In algebraic terms, letting $w$ denote the logarithm of the money wage, $W$,

$$w_t = \phi(N_t, N_{t-1}) + w_t^e, \ \phi(N^*, N^*) = 0, \text{ or}$$
$$w_t - w_{t-1} = \phi(N_t, N_{t-1}) + w_t^e - w_{t-1}.$$

In these terms, $N^*$ is the steady-state equilibrium employment level; since the Phillips function $\phi$ does not contain the rate of inflation, actual or expected, this equilibrium level is the same no matter how high or low the inflation, in which case, following Friedman, we may also call it the natural level of employment.

The concluding point I would like to make here is that, in this model of the labour market, there is involuntary unemployment in Keynes's conception over virtually the whole range of possible employment outcomes. On Keynes's definition, there is a positive amount of involuntary unemployment whenever the situation is such that an increase of demand, by raising the price level, would cause additional labour to be made available to employers at the same or a lower real wage (whether or not at a higher money wage).

Men are involuntarily unemployed if, in the event of a small rise in the price of wage-goods relative to the money wage, both the aggregate supply of labour willing to work for the current money wage and the aggregate demand for it at that wage would be greater than the existing volume of employment. (Keynes 1936: 15)

Then employment would be increased notwithstanding the fall of the real wage. I suppose that Keynes means that the previous level of employment could not have been preferred, so to speak, if the workers would now willingly contribute more effort despite the lower real wage. This has some appeal, and it is interesting that it provides a notion of 'involuntariness' without bringing in what we call job rationing—hence a systematic, endemic failure of the labour market to clear. The only defect of it is that it applies not just below the equilibrium employment level, $N^*$, and even at the equilibrium level, but also above that level and well above it—until, if I am not mistaken, the whole of the frictional unemployment has disappeared! For until the last man is deterred from touring the labour market, an increase of demand of some sufficiently strong dosage will induce an increase of employment despite the possibility that it brings an increase of the price level exceeding the increase of the money wage it induces. (The correct conclusion from Keynes's test is that either the old situation was not preferred, and was chosen through misperceptions etc., or else the new situation is not preferred and is being chosen through misperceptions.) In any case, this semantic matter is not the weak point of Keynes's treatment of the labour market.

Let me now use the above apparatus to discuss, informally and incompletely, some aspects of what I regard as a Keynesian analysis—and hence a non-rational-expectations analysis—of a rather simple example of a disturbance. Suppose that, in a heretofore normal situation, there has just developed the prospect that war might break out any time, say for simplicity an infinitely long war, which, if it occurs, will bring an elevated level of government expenditure. In the event of the war, then, the $q^s$ curve would lie farther to the right, so $N$ would be expanded and $q$ reduced in relation to their normal levels; the crowding out of investment by the reduced $q$ would be insufficient to offset the increased government spending. From any level of $q$ above the reduced war-level of $q$ there is consequently the risk, as long as war has not yet broken out, that war will break out and bring $q$ down; so the prospect that war might break out will immediately reduce $q$ somewhat in anticipation of the risk of the full reduction that war would bring, and $N$ will be somewhat depressed as a result of this anticipatory fall of $q$. The effects are like those of a certain, or deterministic, shift of $q^e$.

A rational-expectations formulation of this problem provides one hypothetical calculation of the anticipatory drop of $q$ and the expectation of its future change. But such a formulation is the impossible fruit of correct knowledge possessed by all and understood to be so. A Keynesian formulation complicates the analysis of $q$ in a couple of ways.

First the Keynesian formulation replaces the (time path of the) known probability of the outbreak of war with the average guess by the individual investors about the true probability of war and, second, it introduces the average guess about the average guess. (There could be further iterations; in principle there is an 'infinite regress' of guesses about the guesses.) The individual's guess about the others' guess matters a lot to him because he will lose more from holding stock in the event war breaks out the lower the others were guessing the probability of war to be, hence the less they were discounting that possibility. In fact, even if it turns out that war never breaks out, the individual will risk more from holding shares the lower is the others' guess if over time their guess tends to move toward the true probability or toward the individual's own present guess; then their under-discounting has greater room for decrease (or their over-discounting has less room for decrease) and the consequent decline in stock prices will be greater (or the increase smaller). So the market for shares will tend to be more depressed than the rational-expectations calculation if either the typical investor overestimates the probability of war or he believes that average opinion under-estimates the probability of war in relation to later estimates and thus leaves that contingency under-discounted in share prices.

In discussing the repercussions upon employment, let us suppose (as proposed earlier) that firms' wage decisions are subject to periodic review, not continuous review, and that all wages are determined afresh every period, not in staggered fashion. Then the rational-expectations formulation might actually predict a rise of wage rates as a hedge by firms against the possibility that the war will break out in the current period (after the firm's wages have already been advertised). In any case, the risk of war prevents wages from falling enough to neutralize the contractionary employment effect of the depressed $q$ during the interval (however long) in which no war breaks out. If war does not break out, then, employment is contracted—a slump; and if and when war breaks out, the fact that wages responded only to the risk of war, not to the certainty of it, indicates that employment will be driven to an above-normal level—a boom. In a linear model, the expected value of employment remains equal to the natural level of employment.

The Keynesian formulation offers considerably richer possibilities. First there is the trivial point that the prospect of war may simply be a phantom of people's imagination. In that case the depressed $q$ thereby induced is none the less real and it will still cause a real slump. Here no one could argue that the slump was the product of the market's rational discounting of the risk of war, however. The subjective expectation of employment, calculated from the subjective probabilities of war entertained by investors, remains equal to the natural level in a linear model, but the objective expectation is definitely down. Second, the labour market will also respond to the added depression of $q$ resulting from the worry of the typical investor that the other investors are under-discounting the unfavourable contingency of war. Hence the slump is intensified by the added depression of $q$. A significant feature of the Keynesian formulation is that, since the participants in the labour market have no way of estimating the average guess about the average guess, there is no ground for maintaining that the objective expectation of employment stays always equal to the natural employment level.

It could be said that all of Keynes is about the difficulties of co-ordination that beset a market economy in which production decisions are left to decentralized enterprises and effort decisions left to decentralized households. Indeed that is the theme on which Axel Leijonhufvud has written so suggestively in his 1968 book and in his subsequent collection of papers, *Information and Coordination*. Any uncertainty on that score was largely laid to rest by the discovery of discarded notes by Keynes, possibly intended for the introduction to the *General Theory*, on 'the contrast between a Co-operative and an Entrepreneurial Economy' and since published in Volume xxix of the *Collected Writings*. However, some thought experiments seem to me to involve problems of co-ordination more obviously or extensively than others. In the previous example of a disturbance, resources did not have to move to reach the new equilibrium; obtaining the wage adjustment to restore employment in the investment sector was the only obstacle to attainment of the equilibrium. Here is an example involving resource reallocation.

Suppose there is a sudden contraction in consumer demand
—a downward shift of the consumption function—of unknown
duration. In the mechanical model, the $q^S$ curve shifts to the
left, driving up $q$ but, in the absence of a drop of the money
wage of sufficient size, contracting $N$. (Two limiting cases,
which are excluded, would be exceptions to this, exhibiting no
effect on employment and no need for a lower wage to prop up
employment again: if the $q^D$ curve—our counterpart of the LM
curve—were vertical, a case of Say's Law, $q$ would keep on
rising until investment was stimulated sufficiently to take up the
slack left by consumption; if the $q^S$ curve were flat, the case in
Tobin's dynamic aggregative model, the drop of employment
would be transitory as the jump of $q^D$ over the unchanged $q^S$
would induce firms to step up their production of capital
goods.) Here I am freezing the expected rate of change of $q$ at
its pre-shock level, say zero. There corresponds to this
disturbance a certain drop of wages that would restore
employment; it is a static sort of problem, and perhaps the
labour market would not require very many months to work it
out. This is especially so if firms have found it not too costly to
diversify operations by having their capital-goods-producing
facilities close to consumer-goods-producing sites. The main
labour-market problems in this case are, first, the familiar
adaptive-expectations syndrome: the worker finds it difficult to
forecast an average market wage over the near future that is
not in the 'ballpark' of the existing or last-reported average
wage; and, second, the intuitive sense of 'hysterisis': when the
average wage drops, the worker is tempted to invest some time
looking for a job still offered at more nearly the old wage on
the belief that there are some lags here and there in the spread
of the general wage cut. Those disemployed workers who thus
for a time hold themselves off the market delay the drop of the
money wage necessary to raise real cash balances enough to
produce the investment stimulus required for restoration of
employment.

The labour-market participants' problem of finding the new
equilibrium wage is complicated a little if financial-market
participants, worrying that the 'good news' of contraction of

consumption (which has boosted $q$) may prove only temporary, respond to initial events by expecting $q$ to begin receding from whatever level it first jumps to. This expectation, hence a drop of $\dot{q}^c$ pulls down the $q^D$ curve, so the intial rise of $q$ is moderated and the corresponding fall of employment is intensified. (This is the counterpart, I suspect, to the sluggishness of the long-term interest rate that Keynes harped on.) If aggregate employment is to be maintained or restored, workers must be willing to accept an extra reduction of wages in order to drive up $q$ by the required amount in the face of the expectation that much of the rise will be eroded. Thus it is possible that $q$ rises little and the wage has to fall a lot.

The labour-market problem becomes much nastier once we recognize that the producers of capital goods are going to fear that the rise of $q$, and hence in the demand price of the things they manufacture, will prove ephemeral at some unpredictable time before they have had time to sell any additional capital-goods output they might decide to produce. In this case the $q^S$ curve shifts up, magnifying the drop of employment while, paradoxically, intensifying the rise of $q$. Thus workers must be willing to accept a still larger reduction of wages to drive up $q$ by the amount required when producers of capital goods doubt the permanence of that level. Imaginably the equilibrium value of the average wage might be close to zero until the pessimism lifts. The wage must fall a lot because of the moderateness of the rise of $q$ that is due to the rise of the demand price and, at the same time, because of the steepness of the rise of $q$ that is due to the rise of the supply price resulting from increased uncertainty. It is not hard for me to believe that the actual average wage would take a few years to traverse the distance from the original equilibrium path to the new equilibrium path.

A rational-expectations theorist would say that there was no serious problem here: the workers need only look at the data on the day or week of impact of the consumption shock— notice the decline of receipts in the consumer-good industries and gauge the decline of $q$—to see the writing on the wall and make the correct forecast of the new expected value of the average wage; and although such a theory is only a severe idealization it represents the best we can do and the most we should aspire to. A Keynesian theorist, I think, would cite the 1982 paper by Roman Frydman which showed that individual agents, if they really act on their understanding of the model in sophisticated fashion, will fail to converge to the rational-expectations equilibrium because the re-estimations by each agent are being continuously contaminated by the simultaneous re-estimations of the other agents; only a simplistic procedure such as least-squares estimation with the expectations of others suppressed would give promise of converging. For a Keynesian theorist, then, the public's expectations about the rate of change of $q$ is an exogenous factor to reckon with, not an endogenous factor, which can be 'solved out', as in a model invoking rational expectations; if the labour market believes that the public may presently become less bearish in this respect, wages will undershoot the mark as long as the bearishness does not let up. Likewise, the increased uncertainty that capital-goods producers will feel about near-future prices following the disturbance to consumption demand is another exogenous factor in the Keynesian perspective. Once we give up the forbidden fruit of rational expectations it is no longer unacceptable to imply, as Keynesian analyses typically do, that wage reductions always, or usually drag out the recovery because they tend to undershoot the mark. Every slump requires learning because each one is different and occurs in an economy of largely unknown structure. The previous generation has not handed down manuals for how to recognize and deal with them all; at best it only teaches what it did in the last slump. Another implication of the failure to converge to rational expectations, it should be noted, is that there will generally exist a diversity of opinion among agents and, as a result (not simply as a cause), a diversity in the kinds of information that agents pay to acquire. The consequences of this for the determination of employment and of involuntary unemployment are only beginning to be investigated.[5]

Another dimension is added to the co-ordination problem if we suppose that any workers disemployed in the consumer-good industries must move to a new location if they are to take up work in a capital-goods industry. Then there may be a hitch over the matter of precisely which laid-off workers relocate and which of them wait for recall to their former jobs (as the recovery of real income brings a partial recovery of consumption-goods employment). In a neoclassical kind of analysis with rising supply curves, there is a unique wage differential between the two sectors such that the required number will move from the one sector to the other. But if that differential is consistent with a large number of workers more or less indifferent between staying or leaving the consumption-goods-making sector, not just the marginal worker (who is indifferent in the non-atomic case), the mere attainment of the new equilibrium wage structure—the fall of the wage in the capital-goods sector and the greater fall in the consumption sector—would not be sufficient to achieve the equilibrium. Too many of the laid-off might linger in the consumption sector, continuing to overestimate their chances of re-employment at the old jobs and underestimating their chances of employment in the capital-goods sector because they overestimate the number of their fellows who are planning to leave. What is needed is some sort of coin flipping to determine who shall stay and who shall leave.

The class of Keynesian research problems I have discussed have as their subject the traverse, to use a favourite term of Hicks's, from the old equilibrium path to the new one. It seems to me that recovery is as much the subject here as the recession itself. In fact the countries falling victim to depression usually manifest a fairly prompt and steady tendency toward improvement. Unemployment rate data from the 1930s show that Britain, Sweden, and Germany had already shown a full recovery from the Great Depression by the time the *General Theory* was published; France and Holland must have been held back by the mounting threat of war. The great exception was the United States, where there were the extraordinary contractions of the money supply well into the decade and the NRA legislation to raise prices. It is true that Europe and much of the rest of the world suffered a protracted depression in the

1980s. But it seems unlikely that this phenomenon is a Keynesian story. To me, the Keynesian theory I have tried to expound here is unable to explain the protracted 1980s slump, but it is well suited to explain the usual recession and recovery.

Keynes himself, of course, insisted that his was a theory that could explain permanent depression—slumps of a non-self-correcting character. It is true that the capital stock may be so large in relation to the labour supply and the technology that no equilibrium will exist (since a non-negative money interest rate is required) until the excess capital has been worked off. But this is certainly a special theory. Another implicit argument is that money wages and hence the price level at some point refuse to fall, the implications of his own theoretical suggestions notwithstanding. He concedes that money wages will be cut with the fall of employment, following a drop in the demand for labour, while making the crucial point that the cut by each employer will not go as far as it would have had the generality of the wage cut been appreciated. But to conclude that the slump will be permanent Keynes must tacitly assume that general wage cuts never become known, as if unpublishable state secrets, and thus will not trigger further rounds of money-wage correction despite the granted insufficiency of the first round of cuts. Finally he makes the lame argument that if wages go on falling the resulting expectation of deflation will only make matters worse. But this side-effect of the recovery process would continue only until the deflation had run its course.

Yet the desire for a theory of permanent slump persists among macroeconomists, and is more persistent than the slumps themselves. One avenue taken is the development of game-theoretical models of a stalemate between the government policy-maker and the private economy. This work is more the creation of monetarists than Keynesians, however, so I will not comment on it here.

Another avenue taken toward such a theory, one which has become increasingly travelled of late, is the construction of co-ordination models in which there exist a multiplicity of equilibria and the possibility that pessimism of some kind could generate a low-level equilibrium. In one group of papers, including a 1982 paper by Peter Diamond on search unemployment and aggregate demand, there is the possibility of a low-employment equilibrium, but there is no involuntary unemployment in any sense. Another kind of model, introduced by John Bryant in 1983, exhibits involuntary unemployment as the result of a self-confirming pessimism on the part of the suppliers of output, who need one another's co-operation. The latter approach is built upon in papers by John Roberts (1987) and by Russell Cooper and Andrew John (1988). This work needs more time to think about than I have been able to give it, so I will not comment on it now.

I would like to point out, though, that the familiar IS–LM apparatus as well as the $q$-type apparatus used above have the possibility of multiple intersections. It follows that the labour market, not knowing which equilibrium the product market and money market will jump to in the upcoming period, will be driven to choose a wage that is a hedge against these possibilities, in which case the low-level equilibrium is indeed one of low employment, not just a low money wage. The labour market will be constantly off balance, not knowing what nominal demand price for labour to prepare for.

It should be acknowledged that the Keynesian view of wage setting, both in Keynes and in my work and that of others, which sees it as a wage-wage process rather than a wage-price process, was dealt a heavy blow in the first oil shock of the 1970s. The wage-wage theory implied that if, as was theoretically possible and perhaps empirically the prevalent case, such a supply shock operates on balance to reduce the equilibrium level of the money wage, two results should follow hand in hand: a drop of employment and a decline of money wages (relative to the recent trend at any rate). Employment did drop, as is well known, but nominal wages actually accelerated a bit. It was a victory for the wage-wage theory that a cut of the real wage was accepted by workers, but a defeat that money wages accelerated at all.

What seems to have happened is that many firms had contractual agreements with their employees, implicit or explicit, that called for an increase of wages when the cost of living increased, contrary to the basic tenets of the wage-wage review. As a result, the contractual view of the labour market received a boost: the real wage became the variable focused on in some models, and in other models the labour market disappeared from sight. I have the impression that some of the new schools of macroeconomic thought that have become visible in the 1980s were spawned by this critical episode in macroeconomic history.

The irony is that, at least in the United States, wage behaviour seems once again to be best conceived as driven by a wage-wage process rather than by a wage-price process. It seems that the indexing arrangements came to be regarded as a blunder by the parties to the agreements. (Perhaps they had intended the indexing arrangement only as a way of protecting themselves against monetary policy or a way of tying the wage to the general level of wages in an era when, in the United States, the wage index was not yet officially published on a monthly basis; then they saw that indexing to the price level was more than they bargained for.) The number of explicit labour agreements possessing clauses indexing wages to the cost of living declined sharply by the early 1980s, and in Japan the imported part of the cost of living was removed from the price index to which wages are tied. It is in part for this reason, I suppose, that the second oil shock, which arrived at the end of the 1970s, seems to have had relatively little effect in most countries both on money wages and on employment. Yet in Europe, where labour immobility is so striking to the foreign visitor, contracts and indexation remain a crucial factor in the behaviour of the labour market.


A few comments on Keynes's policy proposals are in order, not only because they figure prominently in the controversy that he stirred in economics but because they reflect his distinctive theory of the market economy's problems.

The portrait that Keynes's theory drew of the economy, one in which labour-market participants faced daunting uncertainties about the extent of the general fall of wages that will prove necessary to restore employment and about the extent to which other wage setters have reached the same calculation, hardly seems a propitious environment for government authorities to try their hand at stabilization. And indeed Keynes says in the *General Theory* that even optimal policy decisions by the stabilization authorities will inevitably leave a large amplitude of fluctuation in employment. Yet Keynes was no passivist in the battle over policy.

The theory inspired the conclusion that the co-ordination of resources would be improved if the actors in the enterprise system had some signpost that would serve to narrow their uncertainty. Instead of having forty million Frenchmen forever trying to figure out the new equilibrium wage why not have one Frenchman at the central bank constantly estimating the interest rate or money supply (or whatever) needed to make the equilibrium wage adhere to some target path? Barring perceptions that the central bank was making some systematic errors, this target path would give the general wage level for everyone to expect. Thus in the 1936 work we find Keynes suggesting that the objective of monetary policy should be the stabilization of the average money wage. The nearest to a formalization of the argument, I believe, can be found in analyses by Peter Howitt.

Followers of Keynes were left to debate whether it is the rate of change of the wage that should be kept on target, forgiving bygones as bygones, or the level of the wage. Some were content with a variant of the proposal, the older idea of stabilizing the consumer price level. By the time of the Bretton Woods conference, Keynes himself had switched to stabilization of the exchange rate. The rest is history, however unclear its lessons.

## Notes

1. The repeated reading of Keynes, which is perhaps the one sure sign of membership in his school, is an oddity since the members of the other

schools seldom reread (if they read at all) the founder's writings. Another oddity, which parallels an observation about macroeconomics by Robert Hall, is that the American members of this school are concentrated on the American coasts.

2. The algebra of this under-response derives in part from writing the individual's forecast as a linear-homogeneous function of this forecast of the fundamental price and of the others' average forecast, say $f^i(p^*, f)$. Since the forecast function, $f^i$, is increasing in both arguments, it must be inelastic in the first (as well as the second) argument, which was to be proved.

3. It should be acknowledged that, as I would be the last to deny, regarding the expected inflation rate (and for that matter the actual inflation rate) to be a stable function of the employment rate, as my LM equation does, is not generally acceptable. However, it will be harmless for present purposes.

4. It is an analytical slip, it therefore seems, to inject $q$ into an *IS–LM* framework and proceed to ask how the point of intersection of the curves shifts with a shift of $q$, since $q$ is codetermined along with that intersection point.

5. Some analyses of differential information may be found in King (1982), Frydman (1987), and Andersen (1988).

# References

Alchian, Armen (1970) 'Information Costs, Pricing, and Resource Unemployment', in E. S. Phelps *et al.*, *Microeconomic Foundations of Employment and Inflation Theory*, New York: W. W. Norton and Co., 27–52.

Andersen, Torben M. (1988) 'Coordination and Business Cycles', *European Economic Review*, 32, 398–407.

Blanchard, Olivier J. (1981) 'Output, the Stock Market, and Interest Rates', *American Economic Review*, 71/1 (Mar.), 132–43.

Bryant, John (1983) 'A Simple Rational-Expectations Keynes-Type Model', *Quarterly Journal of Economics*, 98 (Aug.), 525–8.

Cooper, Russell, and John Andrew (1988) 'Coordinating Coordination Failures in Keynesian Models', *Quarterly Journal of Economics*, 103 (Aug.), 441–63.

Diamond, Peter A. (1982) 'Aggregate Demand Management in Search Equilibrium', *Journal of Political Economy*, 90 (Oct.), 881–94.

Frydman, Roman (1982) 'Toward an Understanding of Market Processes: Individual Expectations, Learning and Convergence to Rational Expectations Equilibrium', *American Economic Review*, 74/4 (Sept.), 652–68.

—— (1987) 'Diversity of Information, Least Squares Learning Rules, and Market Behaviour', unpublished, New York University.

—— and Edmund S. Phelps, eds. (1983) *Individual Forecasting and Aggregate Outcomes 'Rational Expectations' Examined*, Cambridge: Cambridge University Press.

Goodhart, Charles (1987) 'The Foreign Exchange Market: A Random Walk with Dragging Anchor', LSE Financial Market Group, Discussion Paper No. 0001.

Hicks, John R. (1937) 'Mr Keynes and the "Classics": A Suggested Interpretation', *Econometrica*, 5 (Apr.), 147–59.

Howitt, Peter 'Activist Monetary Policy under Rational Expectations', *Journal of Political Economy*, 89 (Apr.), 249–69.

Kaldor, Nicholas (1939) 'Speculation and Economic Stability', *Review of Economic Studies* (Oct.); revised in N. Kaldor, *Essays on Economic Stability and Growth*, London: Duckworth.

Keynes, John Maynard (1921) *A Treatise on Probability*, London: Macmillan.

—— (1936) *The General Theory of Employment, Interest and Money*, London: Macmillan.

—— (1937) 'The General Theory of Employment', *Quarterly Journal of Economics*, 51 (Feb.), 209–23.

—— (1946) 'The Balance of Payments of the United States', *Economic Journal*, 56 (Mar.).

—— (1979) *Collected Writings*, xxix. *The General Theory and After: A supplement*, ed. Donald Moggridge, London and New York: Macmillan and Cambridge University Press.

King, Robert G. (1982) 'Monetary Policy and the Information Content of Prices', *Journal of Political Economy*, 90 (Apr.), 247–79.

Leijonhufvud, Axel (1968) *On Keynesian Economics and the Economics of Keynes*, Oxford: Oxford University Press.

—— (1981) *Information and Coordination: Essays in Macroeconomic Theory*, Oxford: Oxford University Press.

LeRoy, Stephen F. (1983) 'Keynes's Theory of Investment', *History of Political Economy*, 15/3 (Fall).

Mankiw, N. Gregory and Summers, Lawrence H. (1984) 'Do Long-Term Interest Rates Overreact to Short-Term Rates?', Brookings Papers on Economic Activity (Spring).

Mors, Matthias, and Mayer, Colin (1985) 'Company Expectations and New Information', Working Paper no. 62, Centre for Economic Policy Research, London (Apr.)

O'Flaherty, Brendan (1987) 'Guessing Better than the Crowd how the

Crowd will Behave', Economics Department Discussion Paper no. 347 (Mar.).

Pemberton, James (1988) 'Expectations and Adjustment', *Economica*, 55 (Aug.), 379–92.

Phelps, Edmund S. (1969) 'The New Microeconomics in Employment and Inflation Theory', *American Economic Review*, 59/2 (May), 147–60.

—— (1983) 'The Trouble with "Rational Expectations" and the Problem of Inflation Stabilization', in R. Frydman and E. S. Phelps, eds., *Individual Forecasting and Aggregate Outcomes*, Cambridge: Cambridge University Press, 31–41.

—— (1986) 'Recent Studies of Speculative Markets in the Controversy over Rational Expectations', European University Institute, Working Paper (1987); trans., 'Marches speculatifs et anticipations rationelles', *Revue française d'économie*, 2 (Summer), 10–26.

Roberts, John (1987) 'An Equilibrium Model with Involuntary Unemployment at Flexible Competitive Prices and Wages', *American Economic Review*, 77 (Dec.), 856–74.

Tobin, James (1947) 'Money Wage Rates and Employment', in Seymour Harris (ed.), *The New Economics*, New York: Alfred A. Knopf; repr. in J. Tobin, *Essays in Economics*, i. *Macroeconomics*, Amsterdam: North-Holland, 1971.

—— (1969) 'A General Equilibrium Approach to Monetary Theory', *Journal of Money, Credit and Banking*, 1/1 (Feb.), 15–29.

Wadhwani, S. B. (1984) 'Are Exchange Rates "Excessively" Volatile?' Working Paper no. 198, London School of Economics, London (July).

# 2

# The Monetarist Tradition

MILTON FRIEDMAN, long the leader of the Monetarist school, is intellectually a direct descendant of Keynes and yet a dissenting voice at some important points. Friedman's view of the functioning of the economy and its susceptibility to fluctuations shows a deep appreciation of uncertainty—he would be the last person to predict that wages, following news of a disturbance and data on its impact, will jump so as to neutralize (on average) its effect on aggregate employment—and that feel for the roots of economic instability he inherited from Keynes; he differed here from Keynes only in giving much more importance to disturbances in the supply of money, often the result of the misplaced concerns of central bankers, and in giving less importance to disturbances to $q$. Yet in his analysis of the choice of a stabilization policy Friedman apparently recoiled from a number of Keynes's assumptions and reached policy recommendations in considerable contrast to Keynes's.

The Monetarist movement begins in the 1930s with Henry Simon and Jacob Viner of the Chicago School. Also present at the creation were James Angell and Clark Warburton of Columbia.[1] They advocated that monetary policy follow a fixed rule, such as constancy or regular growth of the stock of money, rather than entrusting it to the discretion of government authorities. Thus they favoured leaving to 'the market' the task of adjusting to shocks. A freely fluctuating exchange rate was part of the preferred system. There was no formal analysis in support of this recommendation. The impetus for this policy position seems to have been a philosophical distrust of government.

Friedman brought to the subject a basic understanding of statistics, and hence of information, learned in his study of biological statistics at Rutgers and Columbia. This understanding culminated in his landmark 1953 paper on the possible counterproductiveness of a policy always aimed at 'full' (or constant) employment. That paper is the veritable magna carta of Monetarism, asserting the rights of market participants to be free of the mischief, however well intentioned, of over-zealous people in authority.

The 1953 paper showed that a continuously activist policy— one that changes the money supply, say, in response to every wiggle in the data on employment etc.—may actually be *destabilizing* in the sense that it actually increases the variance of employment (or whatever variable we use to measure the economic activity in which we are interested). Following Friedman's example, let $y$ be the growth of output, $x$ the growth without an activist policy, and $p$ the growth contributed by the activist policy chosen: $y = x + p$. Friedman then recalls the classic relationship between the variances, $\sigma_x^2$ and the others, and the coefficient of correlation between $x$ and $p$, denoted $r_{xp}$,

$$\sigma_y^2 = \sigma_x^2 + \sigma_p^2 + 2r_{xp}\,\sigma_x\,\sigma_p,$$

to make his point. In order to have the desirable property that $\sigma_y^2 < \sigma_x^2$ it is required that $r_{xp} < -(\frac{1}{2})\,\sigma_p\,\sigma_x$. Thus it is necessary but insufficient that the correlation be negative; a stronger condition is required. This condition might not be met because (1) the data are often highly inaccurate, especially before data revisions, (2) by the time the policy action takes effect it may no longer be desirable. Therefore the 'passive' policy, defined by $\sigma_p = 0$, may be better than any of the activist policies that are apt to be chosen if activism is accepted.

Dagobert Brito (1970) made another contribution to the Monetarist presumption against activism. I think Brito's formulation may owe something to Friedman's occasional emphasis on the 'worst case' in looking at policy, which is reminiscent in turn of Friedman's interest in the lot of the least fortunate in society. In any case, Brito always evaluates things by looking only at the worst possible outcome—the largest deviation of the target variable, $y$, from its target level. If the signal leading us to predict a fall of $y$ below the target level is false—there is no fall, in the absence of action, in prospect—

then taking action that operates to increase $y$ would worsen the maximum deviation of $y$ from its target level. This point leads Brito on to a conclusion involving what he calls the *Friedman zone*. When the observations available to the policy-maker fall inside that zone, the optimum policy, being one that minimizes the maximum deviation of $y$ from the target, is to do nothing. When the observations fall outside that zone, this 'minimax' policy is to respond with an action that will affect $y$ in the apparently preferable direction.

William Brainard in a well-known paper (1967) also made a contribution to the Monetarist stance. The Monetarist premiss is that to put all your eggs in the activist basket—going for the highest average performance—is to adopt a risky portfolio; on the other hand, nothing ventured, nothing gained. Brainard spells out a model in which the optimum policy action is to take a 'small step', because big steps cause too much variance per unit of return. The message differs little in spirit from that of Friedman, though the latter was interested in demonstrating the theoretical possibility that no action would be better than *any* quivering move in the probably right direction.

Much of our uncertainty about how (in both quantitative and qualitative terms) the economy would be affected by an innovation in policy and about how it would move in the absence of an innovation derives from a basic problem of econometrics—the estimation of the coefficients in the correctly specified econometric model. If there were hopes of ultimately achieving a satisfactory solution of that problem—there is little doubt that the American Keynesians held such hopes in the 1960s—they were stymied by the 'Lucas critique' of econometric policy evaluation. The estimated coefficients are chimerical, according to the critique, for if the policy were to change, and expectations of the policy-maker's future behaviour changed accordingly, econometricians' estimates of the coefficients would be systematically altered by the new behaviour of expectations. (The Sims critique of 1980, to which the interested reader is referred, is no less serious.) It is one of macroeconomics' ironies that Lucas, elsewhere a faithful New Classicist, thus worked to rationalize the premiss of uncertainty that underlay the theoretical perspective of both Keynes and Friedman.

The Monetarist analysis of macroeconomic policy setting by the government applies equally to the business policies of profit-seeking enterprises. A firm that raised or cut its price by the amount thought to maximize its expectation of profit with each rise or fall of sales might, in view of the noisiness of its action, actually be adding to the variance of profit. It is possible that risk-averse managers would not welcome the results for this reason even if they could feel sure that their policy was serving to increase average profit. (By contrast, in Friedman's employment stabilization problem it is *possible* to assume that average employment is independent of the stabilization-policy responsiveness, and this assumption seems to be implicit in his analysis; then only the variance or some other statistic (other than the mean) is decisive, the mean being the same.) It may be, therefore, that firms do not respond or under-respond, from the point of view of maintaining expected output and employment, because they feel that taking action or taking more action would be worse for them—not because they are inattentive or not yet at the time of year to attend to those matters.

This point about the reluctance of firms to take collectively the action needed to accommodate, or neutralize, a demand shock, say, would seem to be a serious indictment of the practice of 'leaving stabilization to the market'. But perhaps it only strengthens Friedman's position. Why should the government step in where firms fear to tread—firms which are no angels but which have an interest in stability at least as great as the government's? A closer look at the Monetarist position and its alternatives is needed, however.

In developing a 'philosophy' of stabilization Friedman did not arrive at any conclusions about the kind of system, or *method* of stabilizing, within which to practise the desired restraint. Friedman's 1953 analysis was completely abstract, which led to a difficulty. What does it mean to take no action or to take a small step? Adopting such a policy toward the supply of money might mean causing quite a lot of 'action' with respect to the rate of interest, the exchange rate, and other variables that could be stabilized directly as much as the money supply. Restraint should be practised toward *what*? Nothing was established here about the superiority of money-supply policy over exchange-rate policy or any other kind of policy that a government might feasibly have.

Friedman's best answer to the question, in which he argues that the right answer is to apply restraint to the path of the money supply, is his Presidential Address to the American Economic Association, published in 1968. There, after sketching a model with which to derive the hypothesis of a natural rate of unemployment (to use Friedman's term for it), he points out that there corresponds to it a natural rate of interest (to use Wicksell's term). If the central bank were to try to keep the nominal interest rate stable—or, for that matter, to keep the real interest rate stable—in such a way that the real interest rate is constantly below the natural rate, without any tendency for the discrepancy to vanish with time, the result would be for the employment rate to rise and to remain above its 'natural' level and for the rate of inflation to grow without bound—until the upper bound on what inflation rate the monetary system can support is finally hit, at which point the monetary system would be replaced by barter. The mirror-opposite tendency toward hyper-deflation would follow if the real rate were set above the natural rate. By contrast, a method of stabilization that operates on the (nominal value of the) money supply or on the nominal GNP, rather than on 'real' variables, exhibits no such dangerous tendency toward 'knife-edge' instability. The horror story that Friedman was able to tell in support of this formulation, of course, was the period from 1929 to 1932 when the American authorities kept nominal interest rates low by historical standards but not low enough to prevent a 30 per cent contraction of the supply of money, a shrinkage that must have increased many fold the depth and duration of the 1930s slump.

This problem of choosing a monetary system, or method of monetary stabilization, is far too big to be considered in any depth here. However, a few observations are perhaps obligatory:

1. The proposal to stabilize the money supply suffers from 'vagueness'. It is likely that any given series of actions by the central bank over some finite interval of time could be shown to have 'stabilized', if only by accident, some measure of the supply of money—the monetary base, M1, M2, M3, or whatever. Monetarists, reply, of course, that what matters is the pre-play assurance of private agents that the central bank is going to stabilize some measure of the money supply, lest the economy suffer from excessive and gratuitous uncertainty. But it could be replied that all stabilization proposals display a solemn resolve to stabilize something, and many of them offer the possibility of accountability as much as money-supply stabilization does (for example, exchange-rate stabilization).

2. Lately Gregory Mankiw (1987) and Robert Barro (1988), among others, have been recalling the early literature on the optimum tax on liquidity, or inflation tax (Phelps 1973). They draw from this theory the desirability of stabilizing the tax rate on liquidity, which is the nominal rate of interest; more accurately, the desirability of 'smoothing' the nominal interest rate (much as consumption is smoothed by Ramsey-Modigliani savers). This approach neither contradicts nor falls victim to Friedman's demonstration of the unfeasibility of a constant or insufficiently flexible interest-rate policy. The smoothing proposal would use the ordinary central-bank instruments to achieve expectations of inflation that, in conjunction with the natural rate of (expected) interest, would deliver the programmed nominal interest rate at each date. I suspect that orthodox monetarists would find this proposal too susceptible to abuse by central bankers having ulterior motives to stray from their professed interest-rate objective.

3. The monetarist argument does not by its fundamental nature make a case for stabilization of (some measure of) the supply of money over stabilization of the exchange rate. On the other hand, the advocates of something like the Bretton Woods system have not (in their proposals regarding gold) come up with an attractive proposal for what United States monetary

policy should be. In any case, it would be premature to concede
to the monetarists their contention that the government is apt
to destabilize the economy if its every action is left to its
discretion—if it is not constrained to keep automatically fixed
some of its instruments, such as the money supply and the
budgetary deficit. What is the evidence?

In 1978 Martin Neil Baily published a paper that aimed to
knock the empirical pins out from under the monetarist claim.
Since the so-called full-employment Act of 1946 making
stabilization of the unemployment rate through fiscal and
monetary policy an explicit objective of government, Baily
argued, the American economy has displayed far greater
stability in output and employment than was shown under the
pre-Keynesian policies of the inter-war period. It must be that
the monetarists' scruples against activist, discretionary stabilization policy are ill-founded as an empirical matter.

A few years earlier, it might be added, Phillip Cooper and
Stanley Fischer (1972, 1973) planted some doubts about the
difficulty of countercyclical stabilization by exhibiting simulations
in which a countercyclical policy performed well if it responded
not just with the level of the instrument but with the rate of
change as well (which they called 'derivative control'). Of
course there exist over-aggressive stabilization policies none
the less. This research carried out much of the agenda laid out
in the classic paper by A. W. Phillips (1954).

A little-known paper by Sheetal Chand in 1984 debates
Friedman on his own ground—in terms of the variances and
covariances, or correlation coefficients, that we considered
above. Chand's statistical analysis on American data leads to
the conclusion that Friedman's inequality-condition for the
beneficence of activist stabilization is satisfied. More precisely,
the fiscal activism practised in the United States meets
Friedman's condition for reducing the variance of output. Since
Chand's period of study there has been another test of
discretionary fiscal activism in the United States. If the
defenders of the Reagan policy mix are right, the daring
American tax cuts made when the economy was suffering

withdrawal symptoms at the hands of the Federal Reserve represent another achievement for discretionary fiscal activism.

Yet these important findings do not leave the Monetarists bereft of anything to say. They can cheerfully accept the provisional finding of increased stability since World War II while attributing it more to the success of certain automatic fiscal stabilizers than to the acumen of the US Congress and that of professional government advisers. They can draw a distinction between the performance of fiscal policy and that of monetary policy, arguing that some instruments may have performed a service and others a disservice. They can question the safety of relying upon the intuitive judgements of succeeding public servants over the future. Nevertheless the ball is now in the Monetarists' court.

In recent years a great deal of effort has gone into a more careful construction of the aggregate data. Increasingly it is being suggested that the United States economy before World War II was not less stable, although the Great Depression remains the most enormous deviation from trend. (It could be added that in Europe and several other countries round the world the 1980s seriously rival the 1930s as measured by 'man-years' lost to the slump.) Much of this work is by Christina Romer. A paper by Matthew Shapiro shows that the American stock market since World War II has fluctuated as much as ever, but perhaps that is due to the vigorousness of policies to stabilize output and the inflation rate.

Another response sounds like monetarism but is not. Robert Hall has commented (1978, for example) that fiscal and monetary-policy disturbances are a major source, perhaps on some reckoning the major source, of fluctuations in the American economy since World War II. Some leading examples are the strong rise of employment during the Korean and the Vietnam conflicts, and the marked recessions brought on by the Nixon–Burns and the Reagan–Volcker monetary crunches to curb inflation. To the extent that the most important shocks to the economy tend now to come out of the public sector, not from the private sector, the market-type economy of today is quite different from that portrayed by Keynes. To see the government as more the problem than the solution is congenial to Friedman's world-view. Yet it may be that this transformation has occurred thanks in some part to the complex of regulations and automatic stabilizers and even the discretionary powers of well-intentioned stabilizers on the whole (despite the risks and mixed results) that Keynesians succeeded in introducing into the enterprise economy. In stark contrast to the Crash of 1929, the collapse of stock prices in 1987 left consumers unfazed, their investments in consumer durables on track. This remarkable consumer confidence must have owed something to their conviction that the government would try—and likely succeed—in preventing the crash from causing a serious slump.

Although this discussion does not aspire to be complete, it would leave a void if it did not at least touch on two other Monetarist topics. One of these is the Monetarist theme that a rule—almost any rule—to govern or at any rate constrain monetary policy is preferable to leaving policy to the discretion of the authorities.

The latest case for the use of a rule is not the old argument for a particular kind of rule, or regularity, in monetary policy—namely, the rule of not responding, in some sense, to disturbances—but rather the argument that the optimal monetary policy (and any approximation to it) requires precommitment to a contingency rule. Without that precommitment, each 'generation' of policy-makers will 'assume the worst' about the intentions of future generations of policy-makers, who will have no incentive to please generations prior to them, and draw the conclusion that it must behave accordingly; 'I choose to inflate faster than I would if I thought that by inflating at a slower rate I would cause future policy-makers to inflate more slowly likewise.' (It is a Nash–Phelps–Pollak equilibrium with a faint resemblance to the Prisoner's Dilemma.) For the first-best optimum, the successive generations must be constrained to 'behave themselves' according to a rule. Kydland and Prescott (1977) and Calvo (1978) are the classic references.

An objection to a binding rule is that it deprives the monetary authorities of the opportunity to meet novel and unforeseen contingencies requiring unusual action. Another objection is that, so far, the profession shows no tendency to converge on any one conception of the optimal rule. One man's meat is another's poison. Besides, it might turn out that the choice of such a rule would be made by legislators, the most expert of whom would have a good grasp of some issues but little or no grasp of others. The resulting rule, if actually applied, might be worse than what we had before. Worse or better, there would be the further question of how to enforce it. We have seen that when legislators agree to a self-denying ordinance on the fiscal front they soon enough find ways to circumvent the burden of the rule.

The other great Monetarist topic is inflation and disinflation. Merely to work in this area is almost to stamp oneself a Monetarist.

A grand theme of the Monetarists is that inflation could hardly go very high if the central bank keeps a firm hand on the supply of money. If high inflation has set in, control of the money supply must be regained in order to bring it back down.

The question that has been most researched is what to do with monetary and fiscal policy when a new regime has come to power that is willing to pay the political costs of using those policy tools to bring the inflation rate down in the optimal way. What is the optimal, or least-cost programme? How low does it drive the inflation rate and how quickly?

My work on these questions postulated Philip Cagan's adaptive expectations in arguing that *only* seeing is believing, so expectations of lower inflation will not materialize until actual inflation reduction has preceded them as a demonstration of the government's preferences with regard to inflation. During this necessary stage of learning, in which expectations of inflation are steadily revised downwards in response to the excess of expected inflation over actual inflation, the rate of unemployment will be swollen above its natural level in proportion to the error in expectations. So there must be a slump, though a steadily receding one as learning proceeds. It could also be seen that, on reasonable assumptions, the decline of the inflation rate, after an initial drop, was gradual. The last conclusion was that the optimal target inflation rate would be higher the greater was the discount rate used by the government to weigh future benefits from lower inflation against present costs of higher unemployment.

Now the strategy of disinflation is usually discussed on the premiss of rational expectations, not adaptive expectations. The survey by Drifill (1987) has the references, such as the 1983 Barro–Gordon paper on reputational equilibrium. In this version the expected inflation rate may immediately drop some distance, as the public knows what to expect of new governments on the average, before the government has done a thing. Yet to prove its mettle the government, if a genuine 'reform' government, will establish a still lower actual inflation rate and thus create a slump. In effect, the new work applies adaptive expectations at a lower level—to an underlying variable called reputation—while preserving the main conclusions of the adaptive approach. The new work is in the spirit of New Classical macroeconomics, the older work more in the Monetarist spirit. The former work is a valuable addition, of course. But if one were forced to choose between them, one might pick the latter as better capturing the thinking—or non-thinking—of most persons in a complex and confusing situation.

### Notes

1. A compact history of monetarism is provided in Cagan (1987).

### References

Baily, Martin Neil (1987) 'Stabilization Policy and Private Economic Behavior', Brookings Papers on Economic Activity, no. 1, 11–50.

Barro, Robert J., and Gordon, David B. (1983) 'Rules, Discretion and Reputation in a Model of Monetary Policy', *Journal of Monetary Economics*, 12.

Brainard, William (1967) 'Uncertainty and the Effectiveness of Policy', *American Economic Review*, 57 (May), 411–25.

Brito, Dagobert L. (1970) 'On the Limits of Economic Control', doctoral dissertation, Rice University.

Cagan, Phillip H. (1956) 'The Monetary Dynamics of Hyperinflation', in M. Friedman, ed., *Studies in the Quantity Theory of Money*, Chicago: University of Chicago Press.

—— (1987) 'Monetarism', *The New Palgrave—A Dictionary of Economics*, London: Macmillan and Co., 492–7.

Calvo, Guillermo A. (1978) 'On the Time Inconsistency of Optimal Policy in a Monetary Economy', *Econometrica*, 46 (Oct.), 1411–28.

Chand, Sheetal K. (1984) 'A Keynesian Fiscal Policy and the New Classical Macroeconomics', *Journal of Post-Keynesian Economics*, 6 (summer), 509–22.

Cooper, J. Philip, and Fischer, Stanley (1972) 'Stabilization Policy and Lags', *Annals of Economic and Social Measurement*, 1 (June), 407–18.

Drifill, John (1987) 'Macroeconomic Policy Games with Incomplete Information: A Survey', Economic Research Paper no. 288, University of Warwick (July).

Fischer, Stanley, and Cooper, J. Philip (1973) 'Stabilization Policy and Lags', *Journal of Political Economy*, 81 (June), 847–77.

Friedman, Milton (1953) 'The Effects of Full-Employment Policy on Economic Stability', in M. Friedman, *Essays in Positive Economics*, Chicago: University of Chicago Press.

—— (1968) 'The Role of Monetary Policy', *American Economic Review*, 58 (Mar.).

Hall, Robert E. (1978) 'Comment', *Brookings Papers on Economic Activity*, no. 8, p. 58.

Kydland, Finn E., and Prescott, Edward (1977) 'Rules Rather Than Discretion: The Inconsistency of Optimal Plans', *Journal of Political Economy*, 85 (June), 473–92.

Lucas, Robert E., Jr. (1976) 'Econometric Policy Evaluation: A Critique', in K. Brunner and A. Meltzer, eds., *The Phillips Curve and Labor Markets*, Carnegie–Rochester Conference Series on Public Policy, 1, Amsterdam: North-Holland, 19–46.

Mankiw, N. Gregory (1987) 'The Optimal Collection of Seignorage', *Journal of Monetary Economics*, 20 (Apr.), 327–41.

Phelps, Edmund S. (1967) 'Phillips Curves, Expectations of Inflation, and Optimal Employment over Time', *Economica*, 34 (Aug.), 254–81.

Phillips, A. W. (1954) 'Stabilization Policy in a Closed Economy', *Economic Journal*, 64 (June), 290–323.

Romer, Christina (1986) 'Spurious Volatility in Historical Unemployment Data', *Journal of Political Economy*, 94/1 (Feb.), 1–37.

Shapiro, Matthew D. (1988) 'The Stabilization of the U.S. Economy: Evidence from the Stock Market', *American Economic Review*, 78/5 (Dec.), 1067–79.

Sims, Christopher (1980) 'Macroeconomics and Reality', *Econometrica*, 48 (Jan.), 1–48.

# 3

# The New Classical School

MY topic is the class of models produced by the New Classical school of macroeconomics. The twin axioms of this school of thought are the premiss of rational expectations and the premiss of perfect flexibility of prices and wages (at least the shadow wages used in the firm's lay-off/lay-on decisions). Adherents of Keynes's theory differ from the New Classicals in rejecting the former premiss though not the latter. New Keynesians depart from the New Classicals in rejecting the latter premiss while most of them accept the former. In taking up the pristine case in which neither of the Keynesian 'germs' is present, the New Classicals filled an important logical gap. In the process they reached some findings that have been important to our general macroeconomic understanding—even though most of us would not want to dwell permanently on that special case.

New Classical economics entered on to the scene with two papers by Robert Lucas, one a highly abstract rational-expectations version of the 'island parable' in 1972 and a down-to-earth variation on the same theme, suitable for econometric use, in 1973. Close on their heels was a paper by Thomas Sargent, also in 1973, showing the neutrality of anticipated monetary policy in an intertemporal perspective. Mention might also be made of the 1976 exposition by Sargent. A 1980 paper by Robert Barro began the task of incorporating real shocks, particularly from government expenditures, into the standard New Classical model, although that work served as a bridge leading away from the New Classical paradigm toward the neoclassical theory of the 'real business cycle'. The rational-expectations part of this work was inspired, of course, by the seminal 1961 paper by John Muth and perhaps further stimulated by the 1965 analysis of 'anticipated' prices by Paul Samuelson.

The nature and significance of the New Classical contribution can be gauged only against the background of what had developed before it. Contrary to some impressions the New Classical school did not rise to fame on the suspected futility of monetary policy as a stimulant to employment or the disgrace of the Phillips curve; some pre-existing models had already established the point that a new monetary countercyclical policy would not improve the steady-state level to which the unemployment rate would tend—the natural rate on our theory—and that a policy shift toward a steadily higher inflation rate would have at best a transient effect on employment because the inflation expectations behind the Phillips curve would rise in response.

The earlier 'microfoundations' literature emerging in the last half of the 1960s—the first-generation micro-macro models that introduced expectations into the study of wage-price-employment dynamics—had also addressed the effects of private-sector nominal shocks and monetary-policy shifts. Following Cagan and Nerlove, we worked with the hypothesis of adaptive expectations, applied to the level or to the rate of chance of the variable being forecast. (Muth had shown that under some stochastic processes the rational expectation is in fact adaptive—that adaptive is optimal—so the habit of hypothesizing adaptive expectations had been reinforced.) Consider a permanent shock in the deflationary direction to the level of the money supply or of the demand for money, the permanence of which the actors in the economy cannot at first be sure about. If expectations about the level of the general level of nominal wages are adaptive, we argued, the process of adjustment of the money-wage level would be protracted while people learned to stop thinking that the general wage level was going to revert to its former mean level. Employment, $N$, would remain below its natural level, $\hat{N}$, as long as expectations of the general money-wage level exceeded the actual level (equivalently, as long as actual algebraic wage inflation was smaller than the expected wage inflation rate). In semi-log-linear terms, where $w$ is the log of the wage level and $w^e$ the log of the expected wage level, we have

$$w - w^e = b (N - \hat{N}) < 0, b > 0,$$
$$w^e = hw_{(-1)} + (1-h)w^e_{(-1)}.$$

We saw this modelling as helping to explain the phenomenon of lengthy (yet vanishing) slumps and booms.[1]

When we thought about monetary policy it was usually about disinflation policy, which is in a sense destabilizing in this theory if credibility is a problem, not about stabilization policy. If asked about the stabilizing powers of monetary policy, I suppose we could have replied, 'Clearly, a policy decision, made in response to the unemployment and other data at the end of the period, to institute an *m* per cent increase of the money supply that is going to be announced and, for simplicity, interpreted to be permanent, is implied by our view to be neutral for the equilibrium levels of employment and un-employment—actual and expected wages and prices would jump in equal proportion to neutralize it—provided we work with a "homogeneous" monetary model, as Metzler, Patinkin, and Samuelson explained. But it is not clear to us that an anticipated policy is neutral, for example, a policy that causes the agents to equate $w^e$ to a fixed target, as Keynes proposed.' Before much progress could be made or attempted the New Classicals arrived to dazzle us with their attractive analysis of the rational expectations case.

Although the above analysis is not wrong as far as it goes, the New Classicals discovered another layer of truths offered by the rational expectations variation. To begin with, if the public is unsure about the permanence of the shock it is reasonable to suppose that sometimes the disturbance really is <u>temporary</u>. In the event the shock disappears some periods hence, proving itself to have been temporary, the economy will be in the ironic position of having adjusted its expectations part of the way in the direction of permanence in accord with the mounting weight of evidence that was accumulating until the disappear-ance. With expectations of the wage level below their pre-shock level in that period, the actual wage level set that period will be correspondingly pulled down below its pre-shock level even though the 'demand price of labour' at $\hat{N}$, say $w^d$, is then back to its pre-stock level; that is an implication as long as the wage-setting function, f, makes the firms' wages an increasing function of their expectations of the general level (which they will get to see only after they have irrevocably decided on their own wage), so that

$$w = f(w^d, w^e) < w^d.$$

Hence employment that period will be pulled above its pre-shock level since the firms' labour demand can be viewed as a function, g, that is decreasing in their forecast of the general wage level:

$$N = g(w^d, w^e; \hat{N}) > \hat{N}.$$

The message is that there is no 'systematic' tendency for a prolonged slump to occur after the onset of the shock; there is in each period a chance the slump will continue (with less force) and a chance it will be replaced by a boom (with the odds of the latter growing increasingly long as its threatened severity also grows).

The rational expectations variation had the further implication that if the model is linear the expected value of employment, $EN$, is exactly equal to the natural employment level. This follows from taking the mathematical expectation of both sides of the expectational Phillips relation and noting that, under rational expectations, the wage level that firms expect is equal to the expected value of the wage they will set:

$$b(EN - \hat{N}) = Ew - w^e = 0.$$

The conclusion drawn is that there is no systematic tendency for employment to depart from its natural value. There is never a forecastable slump or boom for if there were wages and prices would have adjusted to eliminate it, much as prices move to eliminate expectable pure profit in neoclassical theory.

The above sketch is certainly a crude representation of the New Classical contribution which has been elaborated with considerable power and generality. Yet I believe that it captures well enough the essence of that contribution so that it can serve as the basis for discussion.

As far as I can see, one does not have any trouble with the first proposition—there is a chance of a boom in the present period (a greater chance the farther the adjustment of the expected wage has proceeded) as well as a chance the slump will continue (with diminished force). It requires us to believe that adaptive expectations arise in response to situations that are stochastic and which people perceive in a probabilistic way; a contrary view is that expectations appear to be adaptive because people are slow to grasp what they are seeing or perhaps even slow to see.

The second proposition, however, rests on a way of thinking that, for me at least, is quite problematic. It requires us to interpret the disturbance—every disturbance—as belonging to a recognizable class of disturbances with known probabilities of continuing or stopping (to keep matters simple as in my example). As was implied in the first chapter, if people do not know these probabilities or if, because the disturbance is *sui generis*, no objective probabilities exist to be learned, it is only the subjective expectations that satisfy the above equalities:

$$b \, (FN - \hat{N}) = Fw - w^e = 0,$$

where $FX$ denotes the subjective expectation of a variable $X$. It no longer follows that the true expectation of employment, $EN$, is equal to $\hat{N}$. It is possible therefore for economies to suffer what might be called probable slumps. But since the first chapter has already complained about the rational expectations axiom in arguing why Keynes should be allowed to live, there is no need to review again the various limitations of rational expectations. Let us go on to examine the New Classical model, with subsequent modifications and extensions, from other angles.

The New Classicals boldly undertook several statistical tests of their model and the early results gave them much encouragement. Subsequent test results rather systematically refuted the early ones, however, and it is not clear how much, if any, empirical support for their model is left standing. (Japan, studied by Parkin, may be the sole exception so far.)

Lucas in his 1973 paper found that countries with a highly variable inflation rate, such as Argentina, exhibited a steeply sloped statistical Phillips curve; since the model suggests that a

high variance in the aggregate price level reduces the responsiveness of output to demand shocks, Lucas took this finding to be
a confirmation of the model. But the 1988 paper by Laurence
Ball, Gregory Mankiw, and David Romer argues that the
steepness of the statistical Phillips curve is related simply to the
average rate of inflation; the authors take this finding to be a
confirmation of the New Keynesian approach, according to
which prices and wages are reviewed more frequently per year
when the average rate of inflation is high, and not consistent
with the New Classical view.

Barro in a series of papers consolidated in Barro (1981)
found that unanticipated changes in the money supply mattered
more for output than anticipated changes, and he took this
finding to be a confirmation of the New Classical model. But
subsequent analyses by Ray Fair in 1979 and by Roman
Frydman and Bruce Rappaport in 1987 found no difference
between anticipated money and unanticipated money, which is
again support for a New Keynesian model, not for the New
Classical model.

A number of economists outside the New Classical school
also undertook statistical tests. Before the rational expectations
variation was formulated there had been estimates of the
proportion of the variance of the unexpected part of the inflation
rate that was explained by the behaviour of the unemployment
rate in time-series evidence. The correlation was generally
found to be negative but the size of the squared correlation
coefficient was typically too small to give much support for the
model either in its adaptive expectations or rational expectations versions. It would have improved the explanation, I
believe, to supplement the level of the unemployment rate on
the right-hand side of the equation with the rate of change of
the unemployment rate, which is a point that is related to the
other test I will mention here. Robert Hall called attention
in 1975 to the phenomenon of persistence shown by the
unemployment: if the unemployment rate was high last period
the best forecast is that it will be high again, though not by so
much, this period; there is a slow 'regression to the mean',
namely to the natural rate, it seems. This was not an alarming

finding for the 'microfoundations' group: their loose specification of expectations did not entail otherwise. But it was a
problem for the New Classical school in view of their prediction
that expected employment was in each and every period equal
to the natural level. Sargent worked free of the problem by
drawing upon the notion of adjustment costs that I had used in
my 1968 paper in order to explain why the Phillips function—
the term with the b above—contains as arguments both the
level and the rate of change of the unemployment rate in a
labour-market environment of sufficient richness. In such a
formulation there is an equilibrium path of the unemployment
rate from the previous rate given by history leading asymptotically to the natural rate (modelled as the steady-state equilibrium
rate); the correct-expectations or rational-expectations scenario
will show the expected unemployment rate moving along that
recovery path rather than jumping to the natural rate in the
snap-back fashion of the simpler model. With the model thus
enriched it was no longer an anomaly that Barro was forced to
use lagged output levels in his explanation of current output.
However, improving the equilibrium features of the model did
not suffice to rescue it from the failure of its predictions about
anticipated money supply changes and, if I am not mistaken,
from its failure to explain to a satisfactory degree the
unexpected component of inflation by reference to the level
and change of the unemployment rate.

All the evidence seems to me to point to the conclusion that
the rational expectationists would have done better to build
upon a model of wage or price stickiness—however fast the
process of unsticking tends to occur and no matter that a
sufficiently big shift of monetary policy would alter that
unsticking process. The New Keynesian theory would have
developed faster and better had all that energy and intelligence
spent on the New Classical model been devoted instead to the
construction of New Keynesian models. The importance of
price and wage asynchronousness—I believe even the word
staggering—had been emphasized in the report of the OECD
committee headed by William Fellner, *The Problem of Rising
Prices*, published in 1965. I turned to the need for a staggering

framework in the final section of my 1968 paper on money-wage dynamics, and somewhat more extensively (in a crude fashion) in the 1970 version, in part because I realized that an announced jump of the money supply would presumably cause a jump of wages, and possibly have no effect on employment, unless some source of stickiness is built into the model. The 1969 paper by George Akerlof gave an attractive example of alternating price decisions by duopolists. So the raw, unfinished ideas were there, waiting to be taken up. The rational expectationists adopted instead the 'island scenario' because, as is often suggested, they were by training more comfortable with market clearing than with job rationing (though we all were, of course) but also, and much more importantly I suspect, because a heavy part of their training and interests lay in econometrics, in which the convention of the period—in fact, the year and the quarter-year—had become ingrained. Had the econometrics of the 1960s routinely used daily and weekly data interspersed with lower frequency data, as many econometricians are beginning to do now, the postulate that in each 'period', hence in each day, all prices and wages are re-established, would have been seen to be the absurdity that it is, and the entire New Classical school might never have had so long a run.

## Notes

1. It is not necessary to delve into the interpretation of the first of these equations—the expectational Phillips-curve relation—to follow the argument here. However, it might be noted that in the market-clearing framework used by the New Classicals, this relation is a structural equation; at least it is glossing over complications of no interest here. But in the present context, in which comparisons are being made between the 'microfoundations' view and the subsequent rational expectations formulation, it is more natural to suppose that, as in the job-rationing models like that in my 1968 model, every firm calls out its above-clearing wage and at the same moment decides upon its employment level, doing so without knowledge of the general level of wages simultaneously set by the other firms. Then one may think of

both $w - w^e$ and $N - \hat{N}$ as structural functions, and hence codetermined by, some notion of real labour demand such as the ratio of the nominal demand price for the 'natural' amount of labour (at the representative firm)—the log of which may be denoted by $w^d$—to the expected average nominal wage. When a demand shock causes the log of that ratio, hence $w^d - w^e$, to become negative (positive), both $w - w^e$ and $N - \hat{N}$ turn negative (positive) as well.

## References

Akerlof, George A. (1969) 'Relative Wages and the Rate of Inflation', *Quarterly Journal of Economics*, 83 (Aug.), 353–74.

Ball, Laurence, Mankiw, N. Gregory, and Romer, David (1988) 'The New Keynesian Economics and Output-Inflation Trade-off', Brookings Papers on Economic Activity (spring), 1–65.

Barro, Robert J. (1980) 'A Capital Market in an Equilibrium Business Cycle Model'; *Econometrica*, 48 (Sept.), 1393–417.

—— (1981) 'Unanticipated Money Growth and Economic Activity in the United States', in Barro, *Money, Expectations and Business Cycles*, New York: Academic Press, 137–68.

Fair, Ray (1979) 'An Analysis of the Accuracy of Four Macroeconomic Models', *Journal of Political Economy*, 87 (June), 701–18.

Fellner, William, *et al.* (1965) *The Problem of Rising Prices*, Paris: OECD.

Frydman, Roman, and Rappaport, Bruce (1987) 'Is the Distinction between Anticipated and Unanticipated Money Growth Relevant in Explaining Aggregate Output', *American Economic Review*, 77 (Sept.), 693–703.

Lucas, Robert E. (1972) 'Expectations and the Neutrality of Money', *Journal of Economic Theory*, 4 (Apr.), 103–24.

—— (1973) 'Some International Evidence on Output-Inflation Tradeoffs', *American Economic Review*, 63 (June), 326–34.

Muth, John F. (1961) 'Rational Expectations and the Theory of Price Movements', *Econometrica*, 29 (July), 315–35.

Parkin, Michael (1985) 'Is the Business Cycle a Keynesian or a Classical Phenomenon: The Case of Japan', Department of Economics, University of Western Ontario (Feb.).

Phelps, Edmund S. (1968) 'Money Wage Dynamics and Labor Market Equilibrium', *Journal of Political Economy*, 76 (July–Aug.), Part II, 678–711.

—— *et al.* (1970) *Microeconomic Foundations of Employment and Inflation Theory*, New York: W. W. Norton and Co.

Samuelson, Paul A. (1965) 'Proof that Perfectly Anticipated Prices Fluctuate Randomly', *Industrial Management Review*, 6.

Sargent, Thomas J. (1973) 'Rational Expectations, the Real Rate of Interest, and the Natural Rate of Unemployment', Brookings Papers on Economic Activity, 2/2, 429–72.

—— (1976) 'The Observational Equivalence of Natural and Unnatural Rate Theories of Macroeconomics', *Journal of Political Economics*, 84 (June), 631–40.

# 4

# The New Keynesian School

THE school of thought that Michael Parkin, writing in 1984, called New Keynesian is a group of theorists who have sought a new wage-price model, or supply subsystem, on which to rest the Keynesian tenets about the effects of aggregate demand and monetary stabilization policy. The earlier 'microfoundations' literature of the late 1960s had contributed flexible wage-price micro-macro models that were presumed adequate as a foundation for at least some of the Keynesian propositions, but the reformulation of those models along rational-expectations lines by the New Classicals so altered the foundation as to make it unfit for Keynesian use: only unanticipated demand shocks had effect over the 'period' (putting aside a qualification of limited applicability), and anticipated stabilization policy had no effectiveness. Those Keynesians not comfortable about dispensing with the rational-expectations specification and even those merely curious to see whether Keynesian doctrine could coexist somehow with rational expectations were therefore interested in continuing the exploration. The New Keynesian models represent a second army—coming in two waves, as I shall indicate—in the continuing push to establish micro-foundations for the Keynesian tenets: the persistence of slumps from a permanent demand shock, and the 'effectiveness' of monetary stabilization policy.

The notion that the average price level and the average wage level are sticky because individual price lists and pay scales are reset at regular intervals on a staggered schedule was an idea that had surfaced in the 1960s, unaccompanied by rational expectations, as observed in the previous chapter. I had the opportunity to present a short paper suggesting that this conception of wage setting might be combined with rational expectations to give some Keynesian results at a November 1974 conference in Minneapolis. It was not until the appearance of several papers in the latter half of the 1970s, however, that the staggering model was made operational and embedded in a general macro model—most of those papers coming out of Columbia, I would like to note.

The first of these papers to come to my attention was that by my then colleague John Taylor (1978), who followed up with a series of theoretical and econometric papers in this vein (1979, 1980). (This paper had in fact been preceded by a paper that Taylor co-authored with me (1977) in which the point is that monetary policy has stabilizing powers if current-period prices are already predetermined before the previous period's shocks and their first-period effects occur, as would be the case if price setting is staggered over two or more periods, but this preliminary exercise lacked staggering.) A paper of mine containing a model of wage staggering with which to examine the existence of a nonrecessionary disflationary monetary programme came out soon thereafter (1978). Guillermo Calvo, also a Columbia colleague, joined in with a series of papers (1981, 1982) in which old prices are never revised but new prices drive the average price level. Meanwhile, at MIT, Stanley Fischer, after some urging on my part, took up this line of research with a wage-staggering model of his own (1977). Later, Jo Anna Gray (1978) and Olivier Blanchard (1983) did work there on staggering-type models. Some related papers from the 1980s will be touched on below.

The way the staggering model operates to make anticipated demand and anticipated monetary policy influential for output is too familiar and perhaps too obvious to need much exposition, I suppose. The practice is to take a model exhibiting the neutrality of money and having a natural rate: more precisely, the steady-state equilibrium unemployment rate and the equilibrium labour force are each homogeneous of degree zero in nominal money supply and nominal prices, and are also invariant to the rate of growth of money and prices, if anticipated; hence money is both neutral and 'super-neutral'. In such a model, a doubling of the money would not affect the steady-state equilibrium unemployment rate. So if the doubling is credibly pre-announced just in time for current wage and price setting to take it into account, and if all wages and prices are flexible, then, on the usual provisos about existence and uniqueness, all prices and wages will at once double and thus neutralize the effect of the money-supply increase on the actual levels of output and employment.

The contribution of the staggered-wage model is to force each firm's pay scale to wait for its appointed time to adjust to the higher money supply. It can be shown that, as a consequence, the average wage level does not jump at first by enough to push up the price level sufficiently to neutralize the increase of the money supply; in a continuous time model the average wage level would be unable to jump at all. Real-cash balances, the corresponding demand price for capital goods, and hence the level of employment will be swollen as long as the price level remains short of reaching the neutralizing level.

It was surprising to me that so many in our profession at first got wrong an important property of the model. They mistakenly thought that the steady-state equilibrium would be reached in finite time—in as many days as it took for all firms to have a turn at revising their wages; in a model where every firm sets its wages once a year, some on 17 February, some on 18 February, and so on, that would mean the boom would be finished in 365 days from its start. Actually the model implies that succeeding wage setters respond by 'undershooting' in relation to the new steady state if the sluggishness of the average wage dampens the firm's enthusiasm for an outsize wage increase more than the fall of unemployment stimulates it. Hence, after 365 days, with all firms having undershot in their first response, it follows that the average wage has likewise undershot. So the boom will have longer to run and, in fact, it can be seen that it will vanish only asymptotically.

I can remember the excitement when Taylor brought back from the Columbia Computer Center the first econometric estimates of the average length of the interval between wage resettings. He let me take a guess. I wanted to blurt out 'twelve months'—all the firms I knew set wages once a year, after all— but remembering John's frequent mention of three-year labour union contracts in the United States I tried my luck with 'thirteen'. The right answer was about eleven or eleven-and-a-half months. There are unions out there, all right, but I had forgotten that there is also casual labour that goes from job to job, perhaps a few times per year. So far as I know, this estimate has not changed very much in subsequent estimations of this kind of model. Note that one could use the estimated model to calculate the theoretical half-life of a boom. I guess that in the United States it is about a year and a half or two.

One might have thought that this model would rapidly become the official model of the league of macroeconomics, at least the US division—a sort of A. G. Spalding baseball of economics. And it did rapidly gain favour in the macroeconomic texts, however muted it remained in some of them. But at the scholarly level the model encountered attacks from two sides: an external attack by New Classicals and an internal rebellion by young turks.

Robert Barro, writing in 1977 almost before the ink of the papers he set out to attack was dry, took issue with the causal connection that the New Keynesians drew, a connection that Keynes also relied upon, between employment and the nominal wage level (as a ratio to the money supply). With the general wage level sluggish and prices in the product market all market-clearing, an increase of the money supply results in a rise in the ratio of price level to wage level at every level of employment; this increase in the marginal profitability of production induces firms to step up their output and employment, according to Keynesian thinking. Barro writes:

Some recent developments in labor market contracting theory [by Baily, Azariadis, and Gordon] have rationalized a sluggish response of wages to changing economic conditions . . . The presence of sticky wages in [the models of Gray (1976) and Fischer (1977)] implies that monetary disturbances can affect employment and output even when the disturbances are recognized, contemporaneously, as monetary in nature. A related conclusion is that feedback rules for monetary policy can be an effective stabilization device. The crux of the argument in the present paper is that [those] models produce that conclusion because the contracting approach is applied only to one aspect of the labor market—wage determination—and not to the other aspect—employment determination. When optimal contractual arrangements are specified for determining employment, the output and employment effects of currently perceived monetary disturbances disappear. In other words, the link between contracting theory and sticky prices does not produce a reconciliation between the standard Keynesian model and rational behavior. (Barro 1977: 305–6)

Many of the New Keynesians virtually invited such a criticism by encouraging a semantic confusion between a contract and what might better be called a commitment. When Harrods or Macys advertises that it is selling a certain product at some specified price, typically for a specified length of time, we understand that the store is making a commitment to sell the product at that price, supply permitting; it is not entering into a contract in the ordinary sense—a contract to supply a specified quantity at a specified price. Likewise, when the store advertises or otherwise makes public and official the wage at which it will hire sales-persons, the store is not offering a specified number of jobs and not thereby entering into a job contract with anyone. Yet these price and wage commitments, which are the stuff of the New Keynesian model, have unfortunately been referred to as contracts by many of the New Keynesians themselves.

Barro's complaint—that contract theory does not support wage stickiness—is misplaced because it mistook the roots of the New Keynesian conception of wages or prices (or both) as long-lived and staggered. The early expressions of this conception had nothing to do with contract theory. These discussions and analyses—by Fellner (1965), Phelps (1968, 1970), Akerlof (1969), and the Cuban economist Pazos—go back at least to the 1960s, and therefore could not have been inspired by the neo-neoclassical model of implicit labour contracts due to Azariadis and company, which arrived in the mid-1970s. Moreover, that model obviously purports to describe a contract expressed in terms of the real wage, not the nominal wage, so it could hardly serve as a basis for a model of nominal-wage stickiness.

The original rationale for the notion that a firm would set its pay scale and hold it there for, say, a year or half-year can be placed under three headings: lead time, decision costs, and reliability.

There are, first, the benefits from lead time in wage setting:

> Presumably a firm would not send out its lads this morning with notices of today's (or even tomorrow's) pay scale to post throughout the town. The reasons have to do with the fact that it takes time for information to diffuse its way through the whole of the potential audience. So the firm can offer less for a given applicant pool if it reaches a larger audience. Also, many workers would be willing to pay something, thus accept lower wages, for having the notice more in advance. In addition, the firm will find the number applying less variable if large numbers of potential applicants are informed of the firm's terms.

So today's labour may have accepted terms offered months ago. Hence the proposition that there is a large element of predeterminacy in the wages which firms today are stuck with. There is no long-term contracting with a person here, only long-in-advance planning.

Second, there are decision costs in wage setting:

> Although the firm could revise its pay-scale plans every day, always keeping some fixed lead time (so that today's decision might apply to the pay scale applying ten working days from today, say), there are obvious savings in managerial attention and information-gathering if the manager makes pay-scale reviews and adjustments only frequently, not daily or hourly or by the minute. (Later we will have to address the issue of the periodic-review model versus the menu-cost model with regard to the timing of these decisions.)

Third, there is the matter of how long the prospective worker can rely on the wage to remain in force:

> Another reason why a firm may find it optimal to establish its pay scale for some significant duration is to enhance the information value of the message. Evidently, a worker would not take note of a wage offer that was to apply to only a certain hour this coming July.[1] In a way, this argument is a

repetition of the second argument except that the set-up costs here are those borne by the consumers of the message.

At this point it is convenient to address the issue of nominal versus real-wage setting. It is clear why firms do not pay their wages in baskets of commodities and gift certificates, let alone in claims to the products, most of them intermediate goods, that the firms are actually producing. But why don't firms express their offers in index terms, with contingency clauses that call for the retroactive adjustment of nominal wages in proportion to the subsequently measured consumer-price index? If they did, it might be argued, firms would understand that an inflationary disturbance they identified as purely monetary and neutral for economic equilibrium was only creating the illusion of wage sluggishness—that there would be a catch-up payment due later to each worker kept on the payroll or added to it, so that added employment was not profitable. The two-part answer to the index question, I think, is this: in the world of *ex post* immobility modelled by the contract theorists acknowledged above, where the worker abandons hope of exit when he signs up with a firm, as in *Mutiny on the Bounty*, it is optimal for the terms of employment to be indexed, and in just the classic way suggested. But the world of the 1960s students of wage dynamics—not only Fellner and myself, the proponents of the staggering paradigm, but also Richard Lipsey, Charles Holt, Dale Mortensen, and virtually everyone else—was one of great mobility. In our view, the firms were beleaguered by competition for their employees, and the chief preoccupation in their wage setting was the problem that too low a relative wage would lead to too large a quit rate. Had we imagined the firms to be so ingenious as to index their wage offers, we would have supposed, as undoubtedly Keynes also would have supposed, that each firm indexed its wages to the general level of wages recorded in the next national report—or if not to the general level, then to the industry level, or to some other parallel wage.[2]

But it would not have been natural for us to portray the firms' wage offers in such index terms. Since a long-run problem of the firm, as we saw it, was to attract a work force in an environment in which it was costly to transmit, receive, and interpret information, the firm might do more harm than good by complicating and encumbering the message it sends about its terms. After all, the firm would have to explain sooner or later exactly how it was promising to index—after one month or one quarter or what? With interest on the retro pay or not? As thoughts of the moral hazards arose in people's minds, the firm would have to specify how the index payments were to be safeguarded against fraud and what protections would be offered in the event of bankruptcy or insolvency. It would seem, therefore, that the individual firm acting alone will not opt for the complexity and the anxiety that the more complex contingent-wage message would entail if all the other firms are sending out messages in the simple nominal-wage mode.[3]

If these reasons for rigidity of a firm's nominal-pay scale between prescheduled wage-review times are accepted, it seems hard to reject the rest of the argument: when demand jumps up, pulling up the firm's market-clearing optimal price—if we confine ourselves now to the market-clearing case—the production manager has no reason to assign himself a higher shadow price of labour (in nominal terms); he has no reason not to reckon that the product wage has fallen and to step up output accordingly. The production manager simply uses the predetermined pay scale in calculating what it would cost the firm to recruit another employee and what would be the cost savings if one less employee were hired or one more fired. The available labour is out there, ready for hiring, since the firm for self-interested reasons is paying above-clearing wages. A similar argument applies to a decrease of demand causing a decrease of the market-clearing price. (It is a banality that if the increase of demand or the decrease of demand is large enough, the firm might deviate from its scheduled wage setting, holding an impromptu emergency meeting to discuss an interim adjustment of its pay scale. Few models are impervious to extreme conditions.)

I hope the foregoing discussion serves to answer reasonably well the criticism that Barro levelled against the New Keynesian programme. One can understand, though, that some theorists will not regard the criticism as truly answered until someone has succeeded in writing down a micro-macro model that serves to support my claims or suitable alternatives for them. I would only want to comment here that it is not apparently inoptimal, at least not to me, that we first try out our theoretical conceptions in the form of working models, to see what their logical implications are and to test them against empirical data, which is itself a considerable investment of effort, before undertaking the investment of endogenizing in a formal way all the new features of the model.

Having defended (at too great length) the proposition that there are long-lived nominal-wage commitments out there in the world, and nominal-price commitments for parallel reasons, we come at last to the proposition that these commitments are typically staggered. It is persuasive, at least to me, that the New Keynesian approach would be of rather limited usefulness in explaining booms and slumps in most countries if, according to the theory, all wage setting were synchronized. Then we would have a situation like the mythical version, whether or not the real version of the Japanese economy according to which all wages are set in the spring—the famous spring offensive; in that case we should not be surprised if we find that the New Keynesian model performs badly, perhaps worse than the New Classical model.[4] The Keynesian tenets would apply, if at all valid, only 'until spring', and would not be evidenced in the data in the months and quarters afterwards.

How to justify the staggering? I remember the efforts of Calvo and Taylor toward an endogenous model of staggering some time in the late 1970s. The essence of their idea was that if all the firms chose to set wages on, say, 1 September of every year, there would be a motive for any individual firm that took the others' behaviour as given to depart from their schedule. The firm would gain from waiting a bit to see what wage or wages the other firms chose. That way the firm would escape the risk, which it would have to bear if it made its wage decision simultaneously with the other firms, that it overestimates or underestimates the average of the wages the other firms have decided upon. Evidently thinking of symmetrical cases, Arthur Okun was led to conjecture what the rhythm of wage decisions would be like:

The likely result of this time-location problem is analogous to that of some spatial-location problems. It generates a tendency to spread the distribution of wage-adjustment dates around the calendar. (Okun 1981)

Fortunately a rigorous analysis of this question is now at hand in the 1988 paper by Ball and Cecchetti. Their context is price setting in an imperfectly competitive product market, and the question to be analysed is whether all firms will make their two-period commitments in the same period, say spring or autumn, or whether they will make their commitments in staggered fashion.

There is a second objection to the staggering model that I said I would come to. This is an objection to the seeming exogeneity of the length of the wage and price commitments. It is voiced more often by those sympathetic to the goals of the New Keynesian school yet worried about its foundations than by the New Classicals.

The result of this concern is a second wave of New Keynesian models, one propelled by the idea of so-called menu costs. The notion that there is a cost to changing the prices on a restaurant's 'menu' is intended as an example, almost a metaphor, for the various set-up costs incurred when a firm goes through the process of altering its price list or pay scale. Among the many significant papers here let me confine myself to citing a small sample: the early paper by Eytan Sheshinksy and Yoram Weiss (1983) showing that the menu cost makes optimal a '*Pp*' price-setting policy function, analogous to the *Ss* policy for inventories; and the papers by George Akerlof and Janet Yellen (1985) and Gregory Mankiw (1985) that argue the proposition that a small menu cost could generate a zone of non-response by wages or prices sufficient to permit a pretty big depression or boom.

Of course, the idea that there are set-up costs—I emphasized the costs of making the wage decisions—in revising pay scales was one of the links in the argument for the staggering model of wages and of prices. But the second-wave New Keynesian economists evidently remained dissatisfied with the idea that wage setting and price setting follow a regular, pre-set schedule, such as every January or every spring and autumn. 'You apparently agree', they argue, 'that a demand shock if big enough will cause a wage or price reassessment ahead of schedule, so why not follow the logic the rest of the way? Proceed to endogenize the size of the gap between actual wage and optimal wage that is just sufficient to trigger a wage-review meeting leading to the immediate posting of the optimal wage—and throw away your embarrassing crutch of a pre-fixed schedule!' So say the young turks (or so I imagine).

Let me reply to this reform movement within the New Keynesian ranks, being perhaps too brief as I have already gone on too long. I believe that it is usually cost-effective for the management of a firm engaged in complex operations to meet the various problems requiring decision by reserving times to deal with them according to a pre-set schedule. There are many advantages in that method. Operating on a regular schedule leaves no possibility that decisions in some areas will be omitted by inadvertence and no need to devote attention to constantly reminding oneself and others of the rising need to deal with that area; it will automatically come on to the agenda when the appointed time arrives. Second, the firm does not then incur the costs of small-scale preliminary studies that seek to estimate provisionally whether the gap between actual and optimal wages or prices currently exceeds the trigger point. There is a contradiction in terms within the argument that since wage setting poses a set-up cost, notably the cost of reaching a decision, let us monitor the situation continuously so that we don't find ourselves making such a decision sooner than is ideal. It means making the decision every day! The firm's timing of its wage (and price) decisions is a second-best problem for which the first-best solution proposed by the new-wave theorists is not optimal in view of the constraints on the decision-time available to the manager.

If it is accepted that these observations are persuasive, at least with regard to some firms, we can see where the new wave errs. Yes, there will exist possible situations in which the suspicion that the trigger point has been exceeded is so strong that the firm will be impelled to make a wage or price review ahead of schedule. But no, that contingency, if it should occur, does not then make it best for the firm to throw away the schedule, the rationale for which remains as strong as ever.

The new wave has nevertheless contributed significantly to the New Keynesian movement by emphasizing that periodicity does not mean an absolutely rigid period—one the length of which is everywhere independent of the growth rate of the expected trend path in the firm's pay and in its prices.

## Notes

1. This point is emphasized together with many other insights, some of them quite original, in the monograph by the late Arthur Okun (1981). The point can also be found, which I had forgotten, in the introduction to my 1979 collection of papers.
2. An interesting paper on this subject is Oswald 1985.
3. Another slant on the same theme is the paper on indexation by Alan Blinder in 1977.
4. Michael Parkin in some work that I believe is still unpublished, cited in the References to Chapter 5, has run a New Keynesian model against a New Classical model on Japanese data.

## References

Akerlof, George A. (1969) *Quarterly Journal of Economics*, 83 (Aug.), 353–74.

——and Yellen, Janet L. (1985) 'A Near-Rational Model of the Business Cycle with Wage and Price Inertia', *Quarterly Journal of Economics*, 100 (May), 823–38.

Ball, Laurence, and Cecchetti, Stephen G. (1988) 'Imperfect Information and Staggered Price Setting', *American Economic Review*, 78 (Dec.), 999–1018.

——Mankiw, Gregory N. and Romer, David (1988) 'The New Keynesian

64      *The New Keynesian School*

Economics and the Output-Inflation Trade-off', Brookings Papers on Economic Activity (spring), 1–65.

Barro, Robert J. (1977) 'Long-Term Contracting, Sticky Prices, and Monetary Policy', *Journal of Monetary Economics*, 3 (July), 305–16.

Blanchard, Olivier J. (1983) 'Price Asynchronization and Price Level Inertia', in R. Dornbusch and M. Simonsen, eds., *Inflation, Debt, and Indexation*, Cambridge, Mass.: MIT Press, 3–24.

Blinder, Alan (1977) 'Indexation', *Journal of Monetary Economics*, 3 Supplement, Carnegie-Rochester Series on Public Policy, *Stabilization of the Domestic and International Economy*, Amsterdam: North-Holland, 128–48.

Calvo, Guillermo (1987) 'Staggered Contracts in a Utility-Maximizing Setting', Department of Economics, Columbia University, Discussion Paper 130.

——(1982) 'Staggered Contracts and Exchange Rate Policy', in J. Frankel, ed., *Exchange Rates and International Macroeconomics*, Chicago: University of Chicago Press.

Caplin, Andrew S, and Spulber, Daniel F. (1987) 'Menu Costs and the Neutrality of Money', *Quarterly Journal of Economics*, 102 (Nov.), 703–25.

Fellner, William, *et al.* (1965) *The Problem of Rising Prices*, Paris: OECD.

Fischer, Stanley (1977) 'Long-Term Contracts, Rational Expectations, and the Optimal Money-Supply Rule', *Journal of Political Economy*, 85 (Feb.), 191–205.

Gray, Jo Anna (1978) 'On Indexation and Contract Length', *Journal of Political Economy*, 86 (Feb.), 1–18.

Mankiw, N. Gregory (1985) 'Small Menu Cost and Large Business Cycles: A Macroeconomic Model of Monopoly', *Quarterly Journal of Economics*, 100 (May), 529–37.

Okun, Arthur M. (1981) *Prices and Quantities: A Macroeconomic Analysis*, Washington, DC: Brookings Institution.

Oswald, Andrew (1985) 'A Theory of Non-Contingent Wage Contracts', Centre for Labour Economics, London School of Economics (Dec.).

Parkin, Michael (1984) 'The New Keynesian Theory of Aggregate Supply', *Macroeconomics*, ch. 25, Englewood Cliffs, NJ: Prentice-Hall, 365–75.

Phelps, Edmund S. (1968) 'Money Wage Dynamics and Labor Market Equilibrium', *Journal of Political Economy*, 76 (July–Aug.), Part II, 678–711. Revised, with Appendix, in E. S. Phelps *et al.*, *Microeconomic Foundations of Employment and Inflation Theory*, New York: W. W. Norton and Co., 1970.

——(1974) 'Remarks on Monetary Policy-Making under Rational Expectations', Conference on Rational Expectations and Monetary Policy, Federal Reserve Bank of Minneapolis, mimeo. (Oct.).

—— (1978) 'Disinflation without Recession: Adaptive Guideposts and Monetary Policy', *Weltwirtschaftliches Archiv*, 114 (Dec.).

—— (1979) 'Introduction', *Studies in Macroeconomic Theory*, vol i: *Employment and Inflation*, New York: Academic Press, 1–19.

—— and Taylor, John B. (1977) 'Stabilizing Powers under Rational Price Expectations', *Journal of Political Economy*, 85 (Feb.), 163–90.

Sheshinksy, Eytan, and Weiss, Yoram (1983) 'Optimal Pricing Policy under Stochastic Inflation', *Review of Economic Studies*, 50 (Oct.), 513–29.

Taylor, John B. (1978) 'Estimation and Control of a Macroeconomic Model with Rational Expectations', *Econometrica*.

—— (1979) 'Staggered Wage Setting in a Macro Model', *American Economic Review Papers and Proceedings*, 69 (May), 108–13.

—— (1980) 'Aggregate Dynamics and Staggered Contracts', *Journal of Political Economy*, 88 (Feb.), 1–23.

# 5
# Supply-side
# Macroeconomics

THE focus of supply-side macroeconomics, like that of monet-arism, is on macroeconomic policy.[1] Supply-side doctrine holds that the prosperity of a country, as measured by current real income or aggregate employment, depends to an important degree on the mix of fiscal and monetary policies followed by the national government. The policy conclusions it reaches (or glimpses) stand in exceedingly interesting contrast to the policy recommendations that are traditional in the monetarist and Keynesian camps.

We do not think of supply-side economics as offering a profoundly original theory of economic behaviour, micro or macro. The importance of incentives, for example, has been the subject of the economists' theory of choice since the arrival of neoclassical theory. Yet in emphasizing some channels and possible responses that were widely ignored by preceding schools it has arrived at a distinctive model of economic activity.

Supply-side macroeconomics is preoccupied with the macro-policy mix. Interest in the mix descended from the observation by Jan Tinbergen (1952) that if a country has $n$ goals and $m$ tools, it will fall short of controllability—of being able to achieve all $n$ goals—unless $m$ is at least as large as $n$; and that is not sufficient, for if one tool has no comparative advantage *vis-à-vis* some other tool the former tool does not really add another independent instrument. One would think that eco-nomists would soon have begun to look at the assignment problem more simply: if you have $m$ tools, optimize—taking into account the thousands of effects of each tool. Instead they began to focus on an interesting managerial problem: if the wielders of tool $i$ are able or permitted to observe only $n(i)$

variables, some or all of which that tool will affect, suboptimize —that is, find the assignment of variables to tools such that if each tool is then operated suboptimally, meaning optimally relative to the subset of effects that its wielders observe, no better result could be attained by any other assignment. This was the famous Hitch–McKean problem in management science in the 1950s that made suboptimal a household word (though when young economists subsequently misunderstood it to mean infraoptimal and proceeded to misuse it that way the original meaning was driven out). In the 1960s Robert Mundell came forward with an influential contribution to this subject (1960, 1962). To avoid an unstable drift of the system away from its steady state it is necessary, if each tool is allowed control of at most one variable, to assign to each tool that variable over which it has its (greatest) comparative advantage.

What we generally call supply-side doctrine in the area of macroeconomics makes its first appearance with the provocative pamphlet on the fiscal-monetary policy mix in the United States that my colleague Mundell produced in 1971. Written against a backdrop of high inflation and high unemployment, the pamphlet argued that 'the correct policy mix is based on fiscal ease to get more production out of the economy in combination with monetary restraint to stop inflation' (p. 24). Thus monetary policy was to be assigned to stabilize the price level or something akin to it, while fiscal policy was to take responsibility for securing a high level of national output. If this paper found a cooler response than was its due, the reason may be that it took a much less short-term perspective regarding the effectiveness of monetary policy for output than was customary; while in so far as its argument that fiscal stimulus would be expansionary was Keynesian in character there seemed to be a contradiction. However, a more nearly conventional treatment by Carlos Rodriguez eventually followed in 1978 which reached the same conclusion about the mix arrived at by Mundell.

Much of the subsequent literature has been stimulated by the evidence from the 1980s when the American economy served, intentionally or not, as a laboratory for experimental testing of the supply-side assignment. Paul Volcker led the Federal

Reserve in a determined monetary attack on inflation while the United States Congress with the encouragement of the Reagan administration legislated successive rounds of fiscal stimulus in the form of reductions in income tax and profit tax rates. In an examination of this evidence in 1985 Jeffrey Sachs found that the speed with which inflation declined in this period exceeded the pace that would have been predicted from the historical relationship between the movement of inflation and past unemployment, and he attributed this performance to the slowing of nominal-wage growth produced (through indexing) by the appreciation of the dollar in the foreign exchange market that the American fiscal stimulus brought about. Although other models and commentaries could be cited, such as the work by Meade and Vines (1987) or the paper by Phelps and Velupillai (1988), the above references constitute the hard core of supply-side macroeconomics.

Several neo-Keynesians—Samuelson in many expositions, Meade, Modigliani, Musgrave, and Tobin to name a few—had pointed out in the 1950s that the various mixes of fiscal and monetary stimulus that would keep the price level on the targeted path are not equivalent in their effect upon the pace of national wealth accumulation. Thus the choice of the monetary-fiscal mix could serve to control within limits both national saving and the price level. Samuelson (1956) is a standard reference.

In their expositions they typically appealed to a static and deterministic model. They held constant the level of government expenditure, this variable being a third tool yet one that is already occupied with the control of a third goal, which is the division of output between private and public goods. If the (degree of) monetary stimulus, $M$, is measured by the money supply and the fiscal stimulus, $F$, is measured by the high-employment government budgetary deficit (often called the structural deficit), the rate of national saving, $S$, and the price level, $P$, are determinable functions of these policy parameters from reduced-form equations. In first-difference form these equations give

$$dS = a_{01}dM + a_{02}dF,$$
$$dP = a_{11}dM + a_{12}dF.$$

On the assumptions that $a_{01}>0$ and $a_{11}>0$ while $a_{02}<0<a_{12}$, hence that $a_{12}/a_{11} > a_{02}/a_{01}$, an optimum policy mix exists: if required wealth accumulation quickens, for example, $F$ must be decreased and $M$ increased. There was no insistence that control should be decentralized in assignment-fashion. 'God gave the Fed two eyes,' Paul Samuelson cracked in a somewhat different context, and the neo-Keynesians often urged fiscal stimulus to pep up employment—to put $P$ back on its prescribed track in the terms used here—when they thought that the adequacy of the monetary stimulus offered by the central bank was insufficient to that task. However, they sensed that $a_{01}$ was close to zero from a long-term or medium-term perspective, and $a_{12}$ might also fade; so much of their discussion tacitly confined monetary policy-makers to the observation and prediction of the price level and fiscal policy-makers to the control of growth.

The framework put forward by Mundell led to a reduced-form system with a different focus. The variables to be controlled by the monetary-fiscal policy mix became the price level, $P$, and the level of economic activity, as measured by employment or production of real income; having in mind the latter two we denote this variable by $Y$. In these terms the reduced forms were

$$dP = a_{11} dM + a_{12} dF,$$
$$dY = a_{21} dM + a_{22} dF; \quad a_{22}/a_{21} > a_{12}/a_{11}.$$

If we take $a_{21}$ as well as $a_{11}$ to be positive, the restriction on the signs may be translated into words by saying that fiscal stimulus via a tax cut (government expenditure being held constant) has a comparative advantage in raising output rather than the price level; the comparative advantage of monetary policy lies in raising (or lowering) the price level.

If $a_{12}>0$, hence Keynesian effects of fiscal stimulus on the price level outweigh the oppositely signed supply-side effects, which Blinder in 1983 suggested was the realistic case, the combinations of $M$ and $F$ giving the targeted level of $P$ lie on a

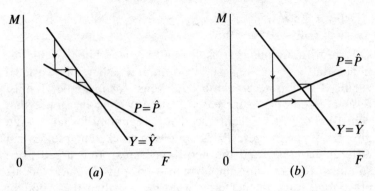

*Fig. 5.1.* The supply-side policy mix yields stability in two cases.

downward-sloping line as in Fig. 5.1*a*. This line is less steep than the locus of combinations giving the targeted $Y$ precisely because a cutback of fiscal stimulus, since it is comparatively effective in expanding output, would require a greater increase of $M$ to restore output to its target than would be needed to put the price level back on its target. But it is also possible that the expansionary effect of tax cuts on the supply of labour would decrease the supply price of output (at the original output level) by more than the expansionary effect on output demand (if any) increased the demand price for output, so that $a_{12} < 0$, as in Fig. 5.1*b*. Here the locus of policy mixes giving the targeted price level is upward-sloping in contrast to the output target locus.

The restriction on the coefficients shown above has the property that the reverse assignment of instruments to targets —the allocation of $Y$ to $M$ and of $P$ to $F$—will lead to an explosive movement of the system away from the intersection of the curves, where both targets are met, unless perchance the policy mix is exactly and wholly right to begin with. The conclusion drawn is that it would be safer and wiser to follow the other assignment—to allot $Y$ to $F$ and $P$ to $M$.

Perhaps it is the case, as Mundell has speculated, that many governments in the 1960s had become accustomed to looking at

GDP and employment when formulating monetary targets while at the same time using fiscal budget austerity as a kind of neo-Keynesian therapy to boost capital accumulation and thereby to flatten somewhat the slope of the unit cost and price level trend. One did hear proposals like that from the more radical neo-Keynesians in those days, whether or not many legislatures were listening. In any case, there is no question that the Mundellian assignment was a heretical dissent from orthodox Keynesian doctrine. It was not so much the idea of reserving price stability for the monetary authorities; after all, the Bretton Woods system of fixed exchange rates already required a country to devote the powers of its monetary policy to stabilizing one price level—the price of foreign exchange—on the theory that so doing would contribute importantly (perhaps decisively) to the stability of the general price level. What was unorthodox was the proposal to stabilize production or employment around some trend path by means of the budgetary deficit when this instrument had already been allocated in the mind of the neo-Keynesians to the control of wealth accumulation—moreover, to boost production by increasing the deficit, not by increasing the surplus (to speed economic growth) as envisioned by the neo-Keynesians.

Macroeconomic policy analysis in the United States was fractured into three warring camps by the early 1980s. The neo-Keynesian camp was attacking the supply-siders for encouraging budgetary deficits that would bankrupt the country and slow its growth. The supply-side camp was attacking the monetarists for their desire for a stable money supply in preference to paying attention to the prices of commodities and foreign currencies argued to have a closer connection to the general price level. Finally, the monetarist camp had not grown tired of attacking the neo-Keynesians for their continuing neglect of the need for operational rules in the conduct of monetary policy. The New Classicals, for their part, kept clucking that it was all a tempest in a teapot since monetary and tax policy were almost neutral. We went from the years of high theory to the years of high comedy, and I think we all enjoyed it very much (perhaps not least of all those in the thick of it).

What are the economics behind the supply-side policy position?
It has been fascinating to me that the doctrine seems to survive
in a considerable variety of theoretical environments.

The supply-side policy mix was initially aired as the solution
to the problem of disinflation. It was explained that a fiscal
stimulus would appreciate the country's currency; the currency
would rise until aggregate demand for gross domestic product
no longer exceeded the output that, given the initial stock of
money, makes the interest rate at home equal to the world rate.
This appreciation would lower costs by reducing asking, or
required, wage rates in so far as workers consumed imported
goods. Thus it would put a stop to the inflationary equilibrium
of anticipatory wage and price increases; and it would actually
increase output since, by increasing the overall real wage
corresponding to the initial product wage in terms of home
output, it would increase the amount of labour supplied. (If this
increase of output is large enough, the money supply necessary
to offset the appreciation might actually increase on balance.)

The implicit model of the labour market here was shamelessly
neoclassical, the real wage being supposed to clear the market
for labour, and the supply of labour apparently portrayed as an
increasing function of the real wage (not by a backward-
bending or vertical supply curve). But on reflection one sees
that a New Keynesian framework, in which a drop of the
'supply wage' would gradually reduce the actual wage by
boosting the unemployment rate corresponding to a given
employment level, would differ in the dynamics but not
apparently in the thrust of the conclusions.[2] One realizes too
that the importation of intermediate goods and capital goods,
the home prices of which would be reduced by currency
appreciation, could also serve as a channel by which an
appreciation reduces costs, so that the Chicagoan supply of
labour curve (which is everywhere upward-sloping) is not
theoretically essential.

The open-economy rationalization was not easily assimilable,
however, by macroeconomists accustomed to thinking in terms
of a closed economy. Moreover, the suggested application of
the new mix to the American situation ran up against the

stylized fact that the US economy imports nothing to a first approximation—and exports less. Another objection that came to mind was the point that fiscal stimulus would not appreciate a country's currency if the major countries of the world were also engaging in like stimulus in pursuit of the same supply-side inflation cure.

So the question arose whether, in inflationary times, the new mix of fiscal stimulus and monetary control of some sort of price or price index could be rationalized as a good prescription for the world as a whole. Is the supply-side, policy-mix proposal right for a closed economy?

Most of the propaganda for the Reagan tax cut did not depend upon the openness of the economy at all and, curiously, much of it was Keynesian in character; it was effective-demand-theoretic, so to speak. The public was told, with utmost seriousness, that the so-called Reagan tax cuts would expand employment by stimulating demand in the same way that the Kennedy tax cut was said to have expanded employment in the mid-1960s. Surely that was a half-truth. The rationale in the minds of the supply-side theoreticians for the preferred policy mix was that if fiscal and monetary policy pull on the aggregate demand curve (in the price-output plane) in opposing and offsetting ways, this shift of the mix will serve to lower the price level (relative to previous trend) and expand output in the bargain (again relative to trend) through its side-effects, so to speak, which will operate to lower the supply price of output. It is absurdist theatre to lionize the right hand for stimulating demand when the left hand is programmed to undo that effect.

Still, in economics matters are often sufficiently complex that what looks at first like a failing answer may finally be seen as having a saving interpretation. Carlos Rodriguez showed in his contribution to supply-side doctrine that if the central bank's announced programme to stop inflation by immediately stopping the excessive growth of the money supply would enjoy full credibility, but a jump of the initial money supply to accommodate the implied declines in the expected inflation rate and nominal interest rate would jeopardize that credibility, a sustained fiscal stimulus can usefully serve as a substitute for that impermissible money-supply jump. To pursue the analogy above, if the anticipation of the left hand's future actions make it desirable that one hand or the other stimulate demand now, and the left hand is immobilized, let us gratefully turn to the right hand for the desired stimulus to demand. Interestingly, the economics profession has not embraced this rationale for fiscal stimulus. Perhaps it is believed that prolonged fiscal stimulus in the form of a long-lasting tax cut, resulting in a large accumulation of public debt, would damage the credibility of the central bank's resolve to forswear inflation as much as the alternative tactic of a one-time jump of the money supply.

The public was also told that the shift to lower tax rates would stimulate national saving. This had its absurd side too since no distinction was made between the effect on private saving, which it is plausible to take as positive, and the effect on public saving—the budgetary surplus—which is very likely, in the case of across-the-board tax cuts, to be negative. Even if such an assumption is empirically valid, however, it is not clear that this mechanism would provide a useful means to disinflation from the supply side, via the capital stock, since a huge change in investment would be required to yield a major reduction of the inflation rate.

The rationale for their policy mix that the supply-side theorists were able to offer in the closed economy case was based on the premiss that the Marshallian supply of labour would be increased by a general tax cut. Their argument was the standard one that the market labour supply curve is increasing in the after-tax wage, so a cut of the tax rate on wage income would increase the amount of labour supplied that corresponds to the pre-tax wage. To that argument they could add the point that even if a permanent increase of the after-tax wage would not increase (or would even decrease) the amount of labour supplied, a temporary increase might have a strongly positive effect because the income (or wealth) effect would be too foreshortened to overcome the substitution effect.

A parallel argument held that what matters is the supply of labour to the market sector, which is where the prices in the consumer price index are. When tax rates are reduced, people are induced to withdraw or reduce their supplies of labour to the underground, or shadow, sector of the economy and to go 'above ground' to the legitimate, market sector. Thus, even if the total supply of labour did not respond to the incentives offered by the tax cut, the redirection of the labour input would have the desired effect of reducing the measured price level. (Even the true price level would be reduced since the distortion of relative prices between the underground and overground economy is reduced.)

Having expounded, as I understand it, the economics of the supply-side position, I would like now to make a few evaluative comments on it, taking it pretty much on its own terms. Later I will try to view the doctrine from a wider perspective.

One of my reactions to this doctrine is scepticism about the quantitative importance of the supposed effects of fiscal stimulus on the supply price (nominal or real) of labour. Take the closed-economy version of the model that I was just discussing. If it were desired to stop a 10 per cent inflation over 5 years, say, how large a tax cut would be required (as a proportion of national income)? After all, in the United States a complete tax forgiveness would not increase the average after-tax wage by more than 20 per cent. This observation does not help to provide reasons for opting instead for the opposite policy mix. But, if accurate, it does suggest that fiscal stimulus may not be the 'magic bullet' to cure inflation without pain or complications that its proponents have sometimes seemed to suggest it is. Huge deficits might be required if all countries were acting in concert to stop their inflations. This would not be so, I can imagine, if there were 'surgical' tax cuts in the right places, rather than across-the-board tax cuts. It appears, however, that legislatures are unwilling to cut taxes unless the benefits are spread widely around the population.

Take next the open-economy version of the argument, which emphasizes that fiscal stimulus appreciates the currency. In fact, in many countries it is argued that a fiscal stimulus tends to depreciate the currency as it arouses fears of accelerated growth of the money supply in order to finance the budgetary deficit. In some countries where fiscal stimulus has succeeded for a time in supporting an overvalued currency, international reserves have run low and the capital inflow from abroad has sooner or later dried up. So it does not appear that the supply-side mix as a method of disinflation is for every country.

Nevertheless many observers have pronounced the supply-side mix an impressive success in its application to the American economy in the 1980s, finding fault only in the slowness with which the overall structural surplus of the American public sector came down in the latter half of the decade. I too am inclined to say that it made a positive contribution to the American disinflation effort. But it is the quantitative aspect of the thing that concerns me now. How much of the success in pulling down inflation per unit of 'sacrifice', measured in 'unemployment years', can be attributed to the policy mix?

First, it is hard to credit all the dollar's appreciation, which figures so prominently in the supply-side case, on the burgeoning fiscal deficit of the federal government in the first half of the 1980s. Most experts in the economics of exchange rates agree that destabilizing speculation was present, driving the dollar considerably beyond what 'fundamentals' imply. Had speculation not lifted the dollar so much, there would have been a less marked slowing of wages than that produced by the actual appreciation. In short, the American budgetary deficit, as a device with which to strengthen the dollar, received reinforcement from speculators, a reinforcement which governments cannot generally count on receiving.

More important, possibly, is the question of whether we have witnessed a causal effect from fiscal stimulus to prosperity in America or whether it is in large part coincidence, a spurious correlation. How much of the wonderful expansion of employment and the remarkable fall of the unemployment rate in this decade can be plausibly attributed to the tax cuts rather than to other factors? In 1988 the structural deficit as a ratio to gross national product—around 3 per cent if we include the heavy surpluses of state and local governments—is almost back to normal; the real appreciation of the dollar is almost wholly erased. Yet the famous expansion continues unabated. 'Look, ma. No hands!' Perhaps this fact is a reflection of favourable real forces, demographic and other, that are entirely or largely independent of the tax cuts.

If one's life study is macro models, one cannot help loving supply-side macroeconomics. It has brought fresh ideas and daunting problems to think about. But, as an empirical matter, there seems to me to be some doubt about the quantitative importance of the channels on which the theory rests.

A severe limitation of supply-side macroeconomics is that it does not offer a full-dimensional analysis of a country's policy mix. There are no foreigners and no future people in the theory, only a pair of reduced form equations in fact. One of the missing dimensions, surely, is any consideration of the effects of the national macropolicy mix upon the choice sets of people abroad—the international welfare dimension.

A serious objection to the unilateral application of the supply-side mix to the American economy when it was suffering high inflation, and indeed to any other large economy in that situation, is that the resulting currency appreciation, hypothesized to be so helpful to that country's disinflation effort, must be held damaging on the same grounds to countries in the rest of the world. Papers written around 1985 by Hans Werner Sinn, Deepak Lal and Sweder van Wijnbergen, and myself, pointed to the United States as the prime source of the record rise in the world real rate of interest and laid the slowdown of the capital stock and the decline in the capital-goods-building industries in Europe to this phenomenon. This hypothesis was the inspiration for the more general Fitoussi–Phelps arguments (1986) showing the ways by which fiscal stimulus and/or monetary tightening in America can produce a slump in Europe and elsewhere.

Supply-side advocates might respond, I suppose, with the observation that the European countries could avoid depreciation of their currencies and perhaps end some or all of their increased unemployment by adopting the same supply-side mix of fiscal stimulus adjoined to monetary policy for exchange-rate or price-level stability. Under a fixed exchange-rate system they would be forced to elect either that mix or one with even greater monetary tightness and less fiscal stimulus (and hence less employment). But some of these countries, such as West Germany and Switzerland, had little or no inflation, so their costs, as they see them at any rate, would have been increased while their benefits would not have been. Furthermore, with regard to countries with the same inflation as in the United States and with the same desires to reduce it, there is still a contraction of their choice set: Perhaps they do not want to reduce unemployment at the expense of future generations in the form of greater interest bills on the public debt.

If these remarks do not miss the mark, it nevertheless does not follow that the Americans are not entitled to any fiscal stimulus whatsoever. But, in principle, the international external effects of fiscal stimulus ought to be calculated and taken into account in some appropriate way in the decision process.

The other political-economy dimension that must be brought into the model is the intergenerational welfare consideration. As practical people, the supply-siders never intended to recommend fiscal stimulus indefinitely; they must have had in mind some gradual shutting down of the budget deficit as inflation grew better and the public debt grew worse. But they never produced a dynamic model with which to study the matter.

There is now some work of a dynamic character by James Meade and David Vines, such as the 1987 paper and a forth-coming monograph. There is also my paper with Kumaraswamy ('Vela') Velupillai (1988). In different ways these two lines of work both make the point that a welfare analysis requires keeping track of wealth—net wealth in the sense of capital in the case of a closed economy and net wealth meaning 'net' of net foreign indebtedness in an open economy.

I cannot do justice to the Meade–Vines work here, and it is best to await their book in any case. I will just mention one of their findings: if the monetary and fiscal instruments are the interest rate and the tax rate, respectively, the path of the mix is determinate only upon specifying the path of wealth.

The results in my paper with Velupillai are surprising and I am not sure that I can rationalize them yet. The problem is to find how the neoclassical conditions for optimum growth and optimum public expenditure need to be altered when money wages or prices exhibit Keynesian pathologies and monetary policy is not able to maintain continuous full employment, being constrained to follow a monetarist or supply-side rule such as fixity of the money supply or of the exchange rate. It is shown that, making suitable allowance for unemployment, the path of national saving in an open economy must continue to obey the law of Frank Ramsey, whose Ramsey–Keynes–Meade rule for the rate of saving every graduate student studied in the heyday of growth theory. But government expenditure must be more expansionary than entailed by Pigou's rule when there is abnormal slack in the economy owing to initially excessive nominal wages. I find this research tough going, but in this direction, I feel, is the way to achieve an ultimate reconciliation of Neoclassical, Keynesian, Monetarist, and Supply-side policy views.

## Notes

1. My terminology leaves room for a supply-side microeconomics alongside the macro. There is a body of literature, stretching from the proposition that marginal tax rates must be zero at the top for Pareto-efficiency, a finding discovered by Saadka and myself in the early 1970s, to the heroic empirical conjecture that a general tax cut would also permit a Pareto improvement, made in the latter part of the decade by Arthur Laffer in reference to the American economy, that is often thought of as 'supply-side micro'. But in truth this literature is indistinguishable from traditional public-finance economics.

2. Under the assumption of a New Keynesian labour market, then, the adoption of the supply-side mix would suddenly boost unemployment while only gradually lifting employment. But the beauty of this arrangement is that the newly unemployed are self-selected, having voluntarily joined the labour force to take advantage of the improvement, presumably temporary, in the terms; they are not selected at random as when firms slow down the speed with which they allow unemployed workers in the factory gates, which would be the result if

the extra unemployment were obtained by a reduction of employment. The former method is cost-effective, I believe, since the extra resources brought into the reserve army of the unemployed in the battle against inflation are those who valued jobs less than those actually holding jobs, some of whom would be laid off by the usual contractionary methods of disinflation. Of course, in richer models there might be lay-offs in export industries as a result of the currency appreciation wrought by the supply-side mix.

## References

Blinder, Alan S. (1983) 'Can Income Tax Increases be Inflationary?', *National Tax Journal*, 26/2, 295–301.

Fitoussi, J. P., and Phelps, Edmund S. (1986) 'Causes of the 1980s Slump in Europe', *Brookings Papers on Economic Activity*, 16/2, 487–513.

Hitch, Charles J., and McKean, Ronald (1960) *The Economics of Defense in the Nuclear Age*, Cambridge, Mass.: Harvard University Press.

Lal, Deepak, and van Wijnbergen, Sweder (1985) 'Government Deficits, the Real Interest Rate, and LDC Debt', *European Economic Review*, 29 (Nov.–Dec.), 157–91.

Meade, James E. (1951) *The Theory of Economic Policy*, London: Allen and Unwin.

——and Vines, David (1987) 'Monetary Policy and Fiscal Policy: Impact Effects with a New Keynesian "Assignment" of Weapons to Target', Department of Political Economy, University of Glasgow, Discussion Papers in Economics, no. 8801 (Oct.).

Mundell, Robert A. (1960) 'The Monetary Dynamics of International Adjustment under Fixed and Flexible Exchange Rates', *Quarterly Journal of Economics*, 74 (May), 227–57.

——(1962) 'The Appropriate Use of Monetary and Fiscal Policy for Internal and External Stability', International Monetary Fund Staff Papers, no. 9 (Mar.), 70–9.

——(1971) *The Dollar and the Policy Mix: 1971*, Essays in International Finance, no. 85, International Finance Section, Princeton University (May).

Phelps, Edmund S. (1985) 'Appraising the American Fiscal Stance', Banca d'Italia, Discussion Paper 56 (Nov.); also in M. J. Boskin, J. S. Flemming, and S. Gorini, eds., *Private Saving and Public Debt*, Oxford: Basil Blackwell, 1987.,

——and Velupillai, K. (1988) 'Optimum Fiscal Policy when Monetary Policy is Bound by a Rule', in K. J. Arrow and M. J. Boskin, eds., *The Economics of Public Debt: Proceedings of a Conference held by the*

*International Economic Association at Stanford, California*, London: Macmillan, 116–30.

Rodriguez, Carlos A. (1978) 'A Simple Keynesian Model of Inflation and Unemployment under Rational Expectations', *Weltwirtschaftliches Archiv*, 114/1 (Jan.).

Sachs, Jeffrey D. (1985) 'The Dollar and the Policy Mix: 1985', Brookings Papers on Economic Activity, 15/1 (Spring), 117–85.

Samuelson, Paul A. (1956), 'The New Look in Tax and Fiscal Policy', Federal Tax Policy for Growth and Stability, US Congress, Washington, DC, Government Printing Office, 229–34. (Repr., Samuelson, *Collected Economic Papers*, Cambridge, Mass.: MIT Press, 1966, Ch. 100.)

Sinn, Hans-Werner (1985) 'Why Taxes Matter: Accelerated Depreciation and the US Trade Deficit', *Economic Policy*, 1 (Nov.), 240–7.

Tinbergen, Jan (1952) *On the Theory of Economic Policy*, Amsterdam: North Holland.

# 6

# Neoclassical and Neo-Neoclassical Real Business Cycle Theory

THIS chapter and the next deal with two schools of thought on the role of non-monetary forces acting through non-monetary channels in the generation of macroeconomic fluctuations. It would be surprising to me if any member of either of these schools believes that, in the whole recorded past, neither monetary disturbances nor the transmission of real disturbances through monetary channels have been responsible for any important fluctuations in economic activity. One does not have to believe that all disturbances to the unemployment rate are in one way or another monetary, as Keynes and Friedman come close to doing, to concede that some are monetary. One need not 'belong' to, or dedicate oneself to, any one of these schools as if it were the sole source of truth.

The impetus for the recent non-monetary research is, I think, twofold. There has been a growing desire to use the advances in methods and concepts of recent years to investigate the extent to which fluctuations can be generated in non-monetary economies, since these economies avoid the conundrums of monetary theory; advances in analysing stochastic processes have particularly animated the classically inclined school. There has also been a growing feeling, strongly fed by the experience of the world economy in the 1980s, that fundamentally monetary explanations of past slumps and booms are in some cases inadequate or implausible; this has especially motivated the other school.

My subject in this chapter is the theory that its developers like to call real business cycle theory, and sometimes 'the' real business cycle theory as if all good non-monetary theory had to be like theirs. The distinguishing feature of these models is their classical style. This classical approach is not another manifestation of New Classical thinking. What was 'new' in that thinking was the incorporation of local, or non-global, information into a general micro-macro model with rational expectations. The 'real-business-cycle' models dispense with that feature altogether. Typically they are, at least from a formal standpoint, essentially classical models of a single-agent economy, and the classical single agent—Robinson Crusoe in the usual treatment of him—does not have the New Classical (and Keynesian) problem of inferring the data in unobserved parts of the economy.

The theory in this new class of models may also be said to be neoclassical because, like the late-classical work of Marshall and others, it contains a choice-theoretic treatment of labour supply and consumption decisions (as well as treating the labour market as clearing, which perhaps all classical models do). Most of these models may be called, to make a further distinction, neo-neoclassical—the added 'neo' indicating that they have a stochastic dimension as found in the later stages of neoclassical theory.

Nearly all the models coming under the banner of real business cycle theory belong to the 1980s: Hall in 1980, Barro in 1981, Finn Kydland and Edward Prescott in 1982, John Long and Charles Plosser in 1983, Robert King and Sergio Rebelo dating from 1986, and by Greenwood, Hercowitz, and Huffman in 1988, to mention some of the main contributions to the group of models I am discussing. (As always, there are so-called precursors, whose only fault was they were before their time, some of whom I cite.) Consequently it is a little difficult, unless one is working in this compartment of macroeconomics, to be sure that one has gathered all the main ideas, so my impressions of the thrust of this research do not necessarily coincide with those of any of the specialists. Nevertheless I will proceed with my provisional perception of this new work and go on to give my tentative evaluation of it.

Since in the theory we are considering the labour market clears and all markets are in equilibrium (in the expectational sense in which I use that term), the 'game' of this line of research is to explain the rise and fall of employment in terms of shifts of the neoclassical supply-of-labour curve and movements along it brought by shifts of the neoclassical demand for labour.

A common thread running through the models in this genre is the shape of the labour supply curve. The suppositions here are the same as those employed by Hicks in the latter part of his celebrated *Value and Capital* (1946).[1] The amount of labour supplied is an increasing function of the current real wage and a decreasing function of the future wage—more precisely, of its expected value. It is also posited to be an increasing function of the expected real rate of interest, meaning that the substitution effect of that 'price' exceeds the oppositely signed income effect. I believe that, in one way or another, every model considered here depends upon one or both of these properties, the current real-wage effect and the current real-interest effect.

For me, three findings are of principal interest.

1. A positive shock, temporary or permanent, to the marginal efficiency of capital—specifically, to present or prospective future rentals on a unit of service from capital goods—drives up the real rate of interest, and in so doing it creates an incentive for managers of capital to run their machinery faster, to gain larger present rentals, at the expense of wearing the capital out sooner. The resulting surge in the services of capital—the revolutions per minute of the machines —shifts up the marginal productivity of labour schedule. This shift operates to increase the amount of labour supplied. (See the 1970 paper by Paul Taubman and Maurice Wilkinson.)

Greenwood, Hercowitz, and Huffman (1988) develop meticulously a variant in which the marginal-efficiency shock takes the form of a decrease in the cost of producing new capital. This has the merit that it militates against a large income effect from the technological improvement; such an effect, by itself, would act to decrease the supply of labour, and since consumption is also thereby increased, the result of the income effect (taken alone) would be a squeezing of investment, hardly a welcome

implication for a model intended
which are typically investment-le

2. A temporary positive shock
capital, whether through sudden
future rentals or through a cro
output by an increase of public o
output of the consumer-goods ind
rise in short and long rates of real
real interest rates is said, as an e
substitution effect exceeding the
supply of labour is thereby increased

My own first exposure to this id ...ᴜ paper by Barro
(1981) on the effects of government purchases. The revival of
the Hicksian emphasis on the real rate of interest, however, can
be traced to the 1969 Lucas–Rapping paper in which a two-
period model of the household's supply of first-period effort
and saving is shown to be capable of generating the desired
real-interest and real-wage effects. Ironically, the paper was
not compelling in its argument that inflationary monetary
disturbances, if unanticipated, would drive up the expected
real-interest rate, but it served to pave the way for models
imputing such an effect to various real disturbances.

3. A temporary positive productivity shock to the marginal
productivity of labour, in raising the real demand price for
labour, has a substitution effect upon labour supply that, if the
shock is temporary enough, must exceed the opposing income
effect. This effect, taken alone, operates to produce a surge in
the amount of labour supplied and thus a transient rise of
employment. It is the economics of the old advice, 'Make hay
while the sun shines.'

This implication of the theory has been the main theme in the
work of Kydland and Prescott and that of Long and Plosser,
and it has been the focus of most econometric tests of the
classical theory.

We could go on to consider additional kinds of shocks and try
to determine what this classical sort of theory implies about
their consequences. For example, it is clear that a negative
shock to the capital stock, as from an earthquake or war, would

ffect that, in a closed economy or one where
pital was domestically owned, would operate to
e demand for leisure as well as for consumer goods,
cause an expansion of employment.[2] An out-of-the-
paper of mine in 1972 pointed out that an open-market
rchase, if it acts like a capital levy, as Metzler argued years
earlier, will expand not only the supply of saving, as Metzler
noted, but also the supply of labour. (Of course, the Ricardian-
equivalence theorem inherent in the single-agent models of
classical-style real business cycle models rules out that 'if'.) But
we have already quite enough propositions to deal with.

I feel that these models comprise an interesting development in
macroeconomics, even if as examples of economic theory at
work they are less than stimulating, and I would not be
surprised if it is finally agreed that some of them are empirically
important, at least in understanding some historical episodes
and some statistical properties of macro time series. (In my
lexicon, if a factor explains at least 15 per cent of something, it
is important for explaining that thing.)

Yet it seems to me that these models have encountered some
serious objections; and while some of these have drawn a
rebuttal, not all of those replies are satisfying.

1. The association of booms with high expected real rates of
interest and slumps with low real rates seems to fly in the face
of the evidence from the extreme observations. The 1930s were
not marked by depressed real—as distinct from nominal—
interest rates (as would have resulted from a negative 'marginal
efficiency' shock). The wartime boom of the first half of the
1940s was not characterized by high real rates; quite the
contrary according to the one study I have seen (Penati 1984).
More recently, the big slump in Europe and most countries
other than the United States in the 1980s was not accompanied
by low real-interest rates; on the contrary, this 'second world
depression' was distinguished by the highest real-interest rates
ever recorded!

If there is a positive correlation between real-interest rate
and employment, I suspect it arises from a high-frequency

relationship that might be most visible in monthly or quarterly data. In view of the historical record just described, it is difficult for me to believe that a positive correlation is exhibited by quinquennial or decadal time series.

2. If we assume for the sake of argument that there has been or will sometime be a depression caused by a negative marginal efficiency shock, the intertemporal substitution model that explains how the reduced real-interest rate could have a positive impact effect on the demand for leisure also tends to predict for the same reasons a positive impact effect on the demand for consumption: the supplies of saving and effort are predicted to fall hand in hand. This observation, first made by Barro and King (1984), follows clearly from the calculus of Lucas and Rapping: it is because the drop of the real-interest rate has made saving less attractive, and saving was part of the motive for working, that the incentive to work is thus diminished. In fact, we do not seem to find any such decline of the propensity to save in the typical slump. Indeed, Keynesians used to say that slumps were often the result of increased thrift.

The contribution of Greenwood, Hercowitz, and Huffman goes some distance toward rescuing the real-interest-shock hypothesis from this criticism. Their argument depends on the influence of the real-interest rate upon the demand for labour, via faster or slower use of capital, not the supply of labour. But one wonders whether this channel is not a rather slender reed on which to rest a theory of the business cycle. The common impression, I believe, is that the elasticity of output, and likewise the elasticity of the marginal product of labour, with respect to capital services is only about one-quarter. In this case, a 4 per cent decrease of services stemming from some drop of the real-interest rate, which would be quite a large decrease, would decrease the real-demand price for labour by only one per cent. This seems too small to explain a slump of significant size and duration. (Remember in any case that the point under (1) remains: statistically, the real-interest rate does not appear to move in the hypothesized way in most or all major slumps and booms in the historical annals.)

3. It seems, then, that the advocates of a classically minded theory of the business cycle cannot escape having to explain how a modest change of the real labour demand price—the real wage that employers are willing to pay for a specified amount of labour services—can elicit a large, perhaps more than proportional, change in employment, at least for weeks or months at a time. The neoclassical rationalization is that the intertemporal elasticity of substitution in leisure is pretty high, greater than one, so small shocks may elicit large rescheduling of working time; but the disutility of working intensifies as fatigue sets in, and the utility of leisure evaporates as a person runs out of things to do, so that the long-run elasticity of labour supply with respect to the real wage is much less than the short-run elasticity. Hall (1988) gives an excellent summary of the claims and a somewhat favourable survey of the evidence.

Yet it seems implausible to say of even the deepest of slumps, with street crime, juvenile delinquency, and all the other social indicators signalling stress, that the decreased employment is correctly viewed as largely or wholly voluntary and indeed an optimal response to the decline of the real labour demand price. The failure of econometric analyses to refute the neoclassical interpretation of the data seems likely to indicate a difficulty in distinguishing between classical and non-classical models.

The fact that several within the real business cycle school have begun to refer to insurance models of the real wage suggests that they also perceive more rigidity in the real wage than is suggested by intertemporal substitutability. Unfortunately, these models tend to have the flaw that they portray those employees laid off as the fortunate ones, and, in the neo-neoclassical spirit, they abstract from the problems of asymmetrical information in labour contracts, which make quite a difference.

4. Critics have jeered at the idea that the ups and downs of employment can be accounted for by the parallel ups and downs of the marginal physical productivity of labour (in the schedule sense, of course). Is it imagined that there is negative technical progress from time to time? A partial answer is that

the derived demand for labour might suffer an absolute drop (not just one relative to trend) for reasons having to do with relative prices: if a future decline of rentals is suddenly foreseen and capital once in place is not shiftable from the capital-goods producing sector to the consumer-goods sector, I conjecture that the neoclassical single-agent economy will respond with a drop of the real-interest rate and a corresponding upward jump of consumption (followed by slower consumption growth than before). If aggregate employment were maintained, employment in the capital-goods sector would drop and so would the real price of capital-goods output; but this reallocation of employed labour would imply a decline of the real value of the marginal product of labour in both sectors, and it is unlikely to be utility-maximizing for our neoclassical economy to respond by moving labour from the former sector to the latter sector in a dogged programme to keep aggregate employment unchanged while accommodatingly swallowing the extra consumer-goods output until the capital stock has fallen enough to permit a resumption of investment at more nearly the normal level. I conclude that, compared to this reference scenario, there will be a drop of aggregate employment and less labour input in both sectors.

5. The more subtle problem with the hypothesis of absolute declines in the real-demand price for labour arises from the fact that there is an upward trend in total factor productivity. Hence, though the demand price for labour (at some standardized level of employment) had dropped by, say 4 per cent, it might well recover to where it had been within a couple of years. How does one explain, say, an eight-year-period in which employment is depressed by, say, 6 per cent or more if in the later years the real demand price has already exceeded its pre-depression level?

I begin to see now that the work at Rochester offers hope of an answer. They posit an aggregate function such as $F(K, AL)$ where $K$ is capital, $L$ is labour supplied and demanded, and $A$ is an indicator of cumulative technical progress to date—the level of the technology, so to speak. If $A$ were to leap up unexpectedly, people would feel poor in relation to their new productivity and accordingly they would work harder (and incidentally save a higher fraction of income); the reverse is true if $A$ drops. A nice feature of this model is that it is not required to suppose that the jump is temporary; in this model it is permanent.

Now ask of this model what happens if $A$ is always expected to rise along some path but there turns out to be an interval of time over which it constantly disappoints—the case of a productivity pause, as I have taken to calling it, that sets back the whole future expected path of cumulative technological progress, $A$. During this run of bad luck the future course of $A$ will always look the same, so on this account there is no reason for employment to turn down or up in relation to its level at the start of the pause. But, over this interval, people will find themselves constantly saving more than they would do if they had foreknowledge and thus gradually accumulating more wealth in relation to $A$ than they would have wished to do. This tendency for wealth, $K$, to outrun $A$ during the productivity pause will induce people to work (and to save) less and less compared to their employment (and saving) at the start of the pause. Thus employment declines absolutely during the productivity pause, not just relative to a rising trend. (As Rochester has shown, there is a utility function such that if $A$ grows at a constant rate as expected, employment will be constant.)

When those in the generation before mine in economics, the cohorts whose ages range from the middle sixties to the middle eighties, are asked to account for their curious career choice they always reply that they belong to the generation that was transfixed by the Great Depression, which struck when they were teenagers or university students or young professional economists. The generation in which I put myself—actually someone once remarked that I was 'between generations'— was not absorbed by the 1930s slump in particular, but we did want to be able to understand the upheavals and pathologies that the world experienced over the first half of the century: the world wars, the hyperinflations, Fascism, Communism, unemployment, underdevelopment. I believe that a lot of us were interested in sociology and philosophy but found economics a more apparently fruitful avenue to the study of society and its problems.

So it has come as something of a shock to encounter the neoclassical real business cycle theory (and all the more so since some of the pioneers are in the same generation, more or less, that I am). The fluctuation of employment is taken up for study in the same spirit, it seems, that one might take up the study of subatomic particles. The research has been a special attraction to people whose main interest is statistics, not sociology or philosophy at all. It is really applied theory—long pre-existing theory—done with new econometric methods, not new theorizing about social relationships in markets, firms, contracts, and so forth. The result is a clash of 'two cultures'.

This clash is epitomized by the vocabulary of the classical enquiry. The word unemployment does not appear. The enterprise evidently wants to exclude the only reason that one has for being interested in fluctuations, namely to understand the mechanisms in the rise and fall of involuntary unemployment. The seeming detachment from substantive interests is heightened by the absence of reference to any real-life episodes and to the words that designate them, like depression and recession; there are only variances and covariances.

Still, the classical real business cycle theory is certainly not without interest to the economic theorist. Lying behind this enterprise, I suspect, is a methodological motive: to show that economics can proceed throughout on the axiom that the world is Pareto-optimal. So one watches in fascination as some of our most brilliant people engage in this odds-defying experiment, and I must admit to being in some suspense myself over how far they will get before it is widely judged that Pareto optimality can go no farther.

### Notes

1. One could also mention the mathematical theory of saving and effort by the single infinitely-lived agent by Frank Ramsey (1928).

92      *The Neoclassical Real Theory*

2. I would like to mention also that some interesting results have been obtained from one-country and two-country real business cycle models by Hian Hoon, a graduate student at Columbia University.

## References

Barro, Robert J. (1981) 'The Effects of Government Purchases', *Journal of Political Economy*, 89 (Dec.), 1086–121.
—— and King, Robert G. (1984) 'Time-Separable Preferences and Intertemporal Substitution Models of the Business Cycle', *Quarterly Journal of Economics*, 99 (Nov.), 817–39.
Eichenbaum, Martin, and Singleton, Kenneth J. (1986) 'Do Equilibrium Real Business Cycle Theories Explain Postwar U.S. Business Cycles?' *Macroeconomics Annual, 1987*, National Bureau of Economic Research, Cambridge, Mass.: MIT Press.
Greenwood, Jeremy, Hercowitz, Zvi, and Huffman, Gregory W. (1988) 'Investment, Capacity Utilization, and the Real Business Cycle', *American Economic Review*, 78 (June), 402–17.
Hall, Robert E. (1988) 'Substitution over Time in Work and Consumption', National Bureau of Economic Research, Working Paper no. 2789, (Dec.).
Hansen, Gary, (1985) 'Indivisible Labor and the Business Cycle', *Journal of Monetary Economics*, 16, 309–28.
Hicks, John R. (1946) *Value and Capital*, Oxford: Clarendon Press, 2nd edn.
King, Robert G., and Rebelo, Sergio (1986) 'Business Cycles with Endogenous Growth', University of Rochester, Working Paper (Mar.).
—— Plosser, Charles I., and Rebelo, Sergio T. (1987) 'Production, Growth and Business Cycles', Department of Economics, University of Rochester, mimeo. (July).
Kydland, Finn, and Prescott, Edward C. (1982) 'Time to Build and Aggregate Fluctuations', *Econometrica*, 50 (Nov.), 1345–70.
Long, John B., and Plosser, Charles I. (1983) 'Real Business Cycles', *Journal of Political Economy*, 91 (Feb.) 39–69.
Lucas, Robert E., Jr., and Rapping, Leonard A. (1969) 'Real Wages, Employment, and Inflation', *Journal of Political Economy*, 77 (Oct.), 721–54.
McCallum, Bennett T. (1988) 'Real Business Cycle Models', in R. J. Barro, ed., *Handbook of Modern Business Cycle Theory*, Amsterdam: North-Holland.
Penati, Alessandro (1984) 'Money, Business Cycles and the Real Rate of

Interest in the United States', Doctoral Dissertation, University of Chicago.

Phelps, Edmund S. (1972) 'Money, Wealth and Labor Supply', *Journal of Economic Theory*, 5 (Aug.), 69–78.

Prescott, Edward C. (1985) 'Theory Ahead of Business Cycle Measurement', Carnegie–Rochester Conference on Public Policy, A. Meltzer and K. S. Brunner, eds., *Supplement of the Journal of Monetary Economics*.

Ramsey, Frank P. (1928) 'A Mathematical Theory of Saving', *Economic Journal*, 38 (Dec.), 543–59.

Taubman, Paul, and Wilkinson, Maurice (1970) 'User Cost, Capital Utilization, and Investment Theory', *International Economic Review*, 11 (June), 209–15.

# 7

# Non-Monetary Theories of Unemployment Fluctuation: The Structuralist School

ECONOMICS was not left out of the modernist revolution that struck the arts and many of the sciences in this century, as remarked in the discussion of Keynes. In economics, one of the most critical of the modernist elements proved to be incomplete information, or asymmetric information (to use the odd term for it that has gained currency). Although Keynes was arguably the first modernist in economics, with his emphasis on imperfect information and expectations of the expectations of others, modernism does not begin to pervade economics until the arrival of Kenneth Arrow. His seminal work on incentive compatibility in the context of insurance contracts became an inspiration for the application of that idea to transactions and contracts in every market of the market economy.[1]

Out of this perspective on the firm and employment relations has come the notion that involuntary unemployment, or job rationing, is systemic to the market economy, at least when operating in labour-market equilibrium (a state in which expectations are correct in the labour market). By now there exist several modernist models of steady-state labour-market equilibrium in which job rationing results because firms have motives to establish real wages in excess of the market-clearing level. The property of job rationing is generally exhibited along the whole equilibrium path, of course, not just the steady state. In some extensions of these models, it will be seen, the path of the equilibrium unemployment rate is 'indexed' to initial conditions and only converges asymptotically to the steady-state equilibrium rate—much as your route to New York depends upon whether you are at present in Philadelphia or

New Haven. In some other versions of these models the equilibrium path is free of initial conditions.

As an aside, I note that this equilibrium theory of the unemployment rate provided solid ground on which to erect the familiar natural-rate theorem: the steady-state equilibrium unemployment rate and indeed the entire path of the equilibrium unemployment rate (from given initial conditions) is invariant to the rate at which money wages and prices are expected to and are actually going to 'inflate' as a result of monetary developments. The models I will be discussing here go all the way in offering an entirely non-monetary view of unemployment.

The involuntary-unemployment models of the steady-state equilibrium unemployment rate, or natural rate of employment, fall into three categories. There is the incentive-wage, or efficiency-wage theory: this theory includes the quitting (or turnover) models of Phelps (1968), Stiglitz (1974), and Salop (1979) and the shirking (or supervision) models of Calvo (1979) and Bowles (unpublished). There is also the notion of a long-term contract between the firm and each employee that arises from the presence of mobility costs, a contract that may also display some sort of incentive feature to ensure that lay-offs are to be deemed involuntary, or unwelcome. And there is now the insider–outsider theory developed by Assar Lindbeck and Dennis Snower, recapitulated in their book (1989). Those models of the insider–outsider type that display a history-free steady-state equilibrium unemployment—and there are some —can be classified under natural-rate theory, at any rate; those that do not evidently present a special case.

In the earliest days of natural-rate theory, especially in the caricatures, the natural rate was regarded as one of nature's constants, like the speed of light. In the infancy of the natural-rate notion it was easy to fall into that mistake since we were preoccupied then with monetary shocks, which were supposed for simplicity to be neutral for equilibrium values of real variables. Moreover, when a big, real-life 'real' shock came along, the oil-price increase of 1974, with its welter of real repercussions on short-term and steady-state equilibrium, we were at a loss to guess what the effect might be on the equilibrium path of the unemployment rate and the natural rate toward which it led; we did not stop to undertake research on the question.

When the need to construct a non-monetary theory of unemployment fluctuation grew stronger in the 1980s the realization dawned that the path of the equilibrium unemployment rate was not generally invariant to real shocks, and that even the steady-state equilibrium rate may be altered by the (permanent) effects of the real shock. The early formulations of the natural rate can now be seen as only the first chapter in what threatens to be a rather long, multi-authored encyclopaedia. Fortunately there is not time to present much more than an outline of this emerging work.

Let me begin by trying to sort out the three approaches to the labour market being taken by the new theory. Then I will move on to the product market and the way these markets interact in the determination of general equilibrium. When we come to study certain kinds of demand shocks and external-interest shocks, it will be seen some interesting novelties and paradoxes are in store.

I do not know (and it seems no one knows) what to call the class of theories, each represented by one or more models, that I am discussing here. Perhaps the term 'structuralist school' will serve well enough, as it indicates the characteristic view that changes in the unemployment rate are the outcome of shifts in the parameters of the model—in time preference, the marginal efficiency of capital, the technology, external prices, and so forth—hence in the structure of the economy. I am not sure how much weight this distinction will bear, but I will sometimes use it as a shorthand label.

While the 'real' school of the classical mode claims the paternity of John Hicks, the structuralist school here can at least claim Hicks as patron saint. That is a Hicks some thirty-five years older and wiser than the fleetingly neoclassical one. In his last monograph, *The Crisis of Keynesian Economics* (1973), he dissociated himself from the Keynesian paradigm of malfunctioning in the determination of the money wage and went on to say that the serious problem in the current-day economy lies in the behaviour of the real wage. The idea of real wage 'rigidity' is often traced back to that book.

What is usually called real-wage rigidity may be defined in terms of a kind of surrogate supply curve in the Marshallian real-wage–employment plane. Following Marshall, we measure employment, $N$, along the horizontal axis, and measure the real wage, $v$, along the vertical axis. For simplicity we take the Marshallian labour-supply curve to be vertical (to a good approximation), and indeed perfectly inelastic with respect to everything unless indicated otherwise; so a movement toward higher employment means lower unemployment and a lower unemployment rate. In response to fluctuations in labour demand, the labour-market equilibrium—located by a point $(N, v)$—fluctuates back and forth along the locus.

In these terms, real-wage rigidity means at least that the locus—variously called the labour-market equilibrium locus, the wage curve, and the surrogate supply curve—is not vertical. Then a drop of labour demand slides the equilibrium point down the locus, causing a rise of the equilibrium unemployment rate along with a fall of the equilibrium real wage. The classic case is a perfectly flat f locus, which might be dubbed a case of pure rigidity. But let us admit the generalized case, a sloping locus, into the fold. (The essence of rigidity is that the surrogate supply locus is flatter than the true Marshallian supply curve.)

Note that, in general, a real shock will shift not only the demand for labour but the equilibrium wage locus as well, more precisely, the relation between the locus and the supply curve, so that the same real wage then corresponds to a different unemployment rate.

This is the simplest type of structuralist model possible. We use it in the same way as we use supply and demand curves. What was, in the early literature, the steady-state equilibrium unemployment rate, or natural employment rate, is here represented by the intersection of the locus and the demand curve. A shock is capable of shifting the demand curve and the locus, thus disturbing the current equilibrium unemployment rate. There is no implication, however, that the equilibrium rate will hold steady after this initial impact of the shock since the demand curve—and possibly the locus itself—may move for some time in response to the gradual adjustment of state variables such as capital and wealth.

Is all this just supposition ahead of theory? Is there any basis for it in any micro model of the labour market? Well, yes, some. More or less at the same time, as so often happens, a number of papers began appearing on the notion of the wage curve. These include papers by Christopher Bean, Richard Layard, and Steven Nickell, the paper by Robert Solow, one by McDonald, and another by Joseph Stiglitz.

The work in which Bean and Solow were authors appeals to the wage-setting behaviour of a union aiming to maximize the welfare of its members. Thus the union wants a certain real wage, $W/P$, and the firm or firms want a certain mark-up, $P/W$. If one or both targets is an increasing function of the employment level, there may exist an employment level low enough to reconcile the two—to bring peace in what Nickell has dubbed the 'battle of the mark-ups'. Actually, all this is quite reminiscent of the formulation by William Fellner of thirty years ago.

The work by Stiglitz appeals to the incentive-wage, or efficiency-wage mechanism. I was a sceptic at first, arguing (at the 1986 meeting of the European Economic Association) that in the quitting model a higher real wage might mean a higher, not a lower, equilibrium unemployment rate as the income effect overcame the substitution effect. Lately I have become aware that some economists feel the same weakness might afflict the shirking story formulation. Nevertheless I have become a cautious convert, in the sense that I would not bet against it. But this model might be able to explain only a very steep locus.

For me the biggest hurdle to accepting this model of the wage locus has been the need to reconcile it with the secular growth of the real wage despite no secular shrinking of the unemployment. Also, relatedly, there is a problem similar to the one that we saw bedevilled the classical school of cyclical theory: if real wages tend to march up at 1 or 2 per cent per year with technical progress and normal capital deepening, any moderate drop of the real demand price for labour will shortly be rolled back by the secular upward trend of the real wage. The best resolution of these two conceptual problems, it has finally struck me, is not the device of postulating technical progress in the home or in the ancestral stomping grounds; the technical progress there has been no match for that in the commercial sector, and such progress there as has occurred—the dish-washers and vacuum cleaners, for example—have been so labour-saving as to have pushed labour out into the market place rather than to have constantly driven up its supply price. The best resolution seems to be the observation that wealth is constantly increasing; hence people are constantly tending to switch toward unpaid work or work with shorter hours or longer vacations unless firms' wage offers keep rising to counterbalance that tendency.

The second conception of the supply side encountered in structuralist thinking puts forward a quite different notion, the idea of real-wage sluggishness, or stickiness. In place of an equation giving the level of the real wage as a function of the unemployment rate we have a differential equation giving the rate of change of the real wage as a function of the unemployment rate. In this formulation, the steady-state equilibrium rate of unemployment may be, though it need not be, itself invariant to some or (imaginably) all shocks. However, if a downward shock to the demand for labour occurs, the failure of the current real wage to budge on impact means that in effect we have a perfectly flat wage locus: the unemployment rate jumps up while the real wage does not jump at all—it only begins its slow decline in response to the increased level of unemployment.

There is no fully developed micro-theoretic model on which to rest this type of real-wage behaviour. As hinted at before, one can imagine a contractual model based on large mobility costs: each worker chooses an employer for life, and before making that long journey from which there is no return he obtains a lifetime contract stipulating the wage when laid off and the wage when laid on; the problem for the firm is to write the contract in such a way that the employee has the profit-maximizing degree of incentive to stay in shape so as to be ready at all times to be called up. When a red alert occurs and the employees are scrambled, the firm does not want to find any employees unable to perform tolerably close to peak form. If a shock reduced the real-demand price for labour, that is, the expected path of the shadow price of active labour input falls, the firm cannot alter the contracts of existing employees, but it can immediately begin offering less attractive terms to new recruits. With time, then, the cost to the firm of laying on an additional day or hour of labour input declines.

What theoretical work exists on this sort of model? Nothing at all of which I am aware. I plan to try to develop a model of this kind myself. Certainly there are going to be stumbling blocks to a satisfactory realization of such a model, though. This is a model in which the young auction themselves off to the lifetime employers, so there is no youth unemployment of the familiar sort. All the unemployment takes the form of underutilization of paid employees by their employers. (Those laid off would be glad to accept a reduced wage in the laid-on status but cannot persuade their employers that such a narrowing of the differential would be cost-effective, since it would not be judged compatible with the workers' incentive to shirk or to let their readiness atrophy when laid off.) Yet this is a kind of unemployment, it is reflected in reduced earnings, and it may be concentrated among the junior employees.

It is probably clear how this model works in conjunction with the demand side. A negative shock to the real-demand price of labour, although it causes the unemployment rate to jump up, does set in motion one sort of self-correcting mechanism; for with increased unemployment the real wage will be constantly falling, so that the labour-market equilibrium will be tending to slide downwards and therefore rightwards along the demand curve. Unless the demand curve itself is dropping faster than that, there will be a tendency for recovery to the (possibly unaltered) steady-state equilibrium unemployment rate.

The third treatment of the supply side found in structuralist models is that provided by the insider–outsider view of unemployment. The key idea here is that the 'insiders', who are those employed in the previous 'period' and possibly those just hired to replace retirees whose inputs were sufficiently valuable to retain, will push up the wage as high as it will go within the constraint that they do not thereby cause the firm, which maintains autonomy over aggregate manning, to reduce the number of employees; hence the wage is equated to the real-demand price of labour that is expected at the start of the current period. (No account is taken of risk here, I think.) An implication is that if an adverse demand shock has caused last period's employment to fall, and demand this period is expected to remain at the same depressed level, the union will not be prompted by the fall of employment to cut the real wage it requires. (The firm must have cut employment by just the amount needed to keep the demand price equal to wage.) Thus recovery is not helped. Further, if demand is expected to recover somewhat, the union will respond by sharply increasing its real-wage requirement this period. In this case recovery is actually repelled by the militant wage increase. Variants of this view, such as bargaining models and seniority models, tend to give broadly similar results.

Among the papers that might be cited here, besides the large volume of work by Lindbeck and Snower already mentioned, is a paper by Robert Hall foreshadowing the insider–outsider theory written in 1970 (which I discussed in my 1972 book when coming to the subject of hysterisis). Some other recent work of importance is by Nils Gottfries and Hendrik Horn (1987), Allen Drazen and Nils Gottfries (1987), Andrew Oswald (1985), and Olivier Blanchard and Lawrence Summers (1986*a* and *b*).

The reason this work has caused excitement, more than theoretical models usually do no matter how innovative, is that their appearance has coincided with statistical investigations finding that unemployment in Europe, and since World War II also in the United States, displays what has come to be called hysterisis: the current period's equilibrium unemployment rate is not history-free but, rather, depends upon the history of the unemployment rate in the previous period. The insider–outsider approach can explain why last period's depression, the causes of which are no longer to be seen, seems to place a heavy hand on equilibrium in the present. The second group of models also says that yesterday is a good forecast of today if, but only if, yesterday's shock carries over to today. The economists doing the statistical work say they see hysterisis in the data. What are non-statisticians to say? Certainly I cannot see hysterisis with the naked eye. I know that unemployment is still high in Europe, but I also know that, until fairly recently, the real rate of interest in New York and Hong Kong was still fairly elevated above its normal level; so I am not totally surprised not to see a full recovery in Europe by this point. On the other hand, I cannot see the absence of hysterisis with any clarity either. I suppose that we should concede the strong likelihood that there is a degree of hysterisis present, and therefore be glad that we have the insider–outsider models as an important contribution to the set of reasons why, following the onset and subsequent remission of a negative shock, recovery takes quite a while.

A curmudgeonly listener to this survey might say that it is all very interesting but it is only as good as our theory of how real shocks shift the real-demand price for labour (or shift the equilibrium locus in the case of the first group of models). Certainly we saw that the neoclassical theory does not have an easy time explaining how real shocks, operating through neoclassical channels, can be large enough to do much damage. So the question arises here: what kinds of shock can disturb the equilibrium path of the unemployment rate, by what channels do they operate, and are they of potential empirical importance —particularly in real-life historical episodes, such as Europe in the 1980s.

Much depends upon how we model the product markets. The textbook treatments of aggregate supply—usually discussion of the aggregate production function and the conditions obtaining under pure competition and imperfect competition— certainly present rather limited opportunities for shocks to disturb the real-demand price for labour. Nevertheless, this framework was able to be used for the analysis of the effect of an oil shock on domestic employment of an open economy by Michael Bruno and Jeffrey Sachs (1985). They went on to consider the effects of an adverse change in the terms of trade, which means that the country's product wage must increase if it is to offer the same real wage (in terms of the basket of consumer goods demanded by workers). These two are perhaps the pioneers in the use of structuralist models to explain the decline of employment in the mid-1970s and in the early part of the next decade.[2]

Some recent work of mine has sought to recast some of the models in the Fitoussi–Phelps monograph (1988) into models of the non-monetary, structuralist type I am reviewing here. One of these themes is the effect of an external real-interest shock upon domestic employment in an open economy. Our idea was that the supply price of output, say $P/W$ if measured in labour units, at a specified level of employment is an increasing function of the real interest rate, taking actual and expected rates to be equal.

This real-interest effect is clear if the economy's products consist of both a consumer good and a capital good, and the latter is taken to be non-tradeable (which some capital goods, such as construction, tend to be). It is a relatively simple exercise to show (Phelps 1988*a*) that if the open economy is small, and thus takes the world real-interest rate as given, a positive shock to the real rate will drive down the real-demand price—the price in terms of the consumer good—of the output of the capital-good producing sector, causing employment to fall. Aggregate employment could be maintained, given the new relative price, only if producers were offered an increased price in terms of labour—a higher $P/W$—for consumer-good output. Thus the higher real interest rate may be said to have contracted supply.

Surprisingly, I think, it was possible to show similar

consequences when the positive disturbance to the real-interest rate, rather than being an external shock of an exogenous nature, was the endogenous result of an upward shock to consumption demand; the latter might be a disturbance induced by a 'helicopter drop' of additional government debt on the economy or it might be the outcome of an autonomous upward shift in the rate of pure time preference. The increased consumption demand is unable to generate increased employment in the consumer-good producing sector, since the set-up on the real-wage front makes additional output there unprofitable under existing real-wage conditions, so the only way the excess demand for consumption goods can be eliminated is through a drop in the real price of the capital good; this is similar to an upward shift of the path of the (instantaneous) real-interest rate, and its effect is clearly to reduce the amount of output that producers of the capital good are willing to supply.

Another model of the product market that has the same possibilities with regard to real-interest shocks is the customer market model, in particular the early formulation by Sidney Winter and myself in 1970. In a recent paper (1988c) I showed that a positive disturbance to the real-interest rate in a closed economy, originating in either of the ways indicated above, would depress employment even when there is no capital-good producing sector whose output responds the 'wrong way' to consumers' exuberance. The key to that result is that the firms' desired mark-up over wage costs at a specified level of employment is an increasing function of the real-interest rate path—equivalently, a decreasing function of the shadow price of customers, which drops when consumption demand drives up real-interest rates and drives down share prices.

As suggested above, these models will deliver the short-term consequences for employment just indicated no matter which of the three labour-market models is hooked up to the product-market model. However, the longer-run response of employment will evidently depend upon which of those three labour-market models is chosen. Clearly the sticky real-wage model offers the possibility of a full recovery of the unemployment rate—to a possibly unaltered steady-state equilibrium un-employment rate. By contrast, the wage-locus model seems to be gloomy about the prospects of a full recovery. Finally, it is not clear what the long run brings in an insider–outsider model without a further specification of employer behaviour.

Other shocks can be analysed, of course, and will be. The reason that consumption shocks, in both one- and two-country models, are especially interesting at this time is that the past decade has witnessed a spectacular surge of budgetary deficits in the world, some of them induced by the decline of economic activity but others, notably that in the United States, the result of a policy shock—the tax cuts in the first half of the 1980s.

The virtue of this approach is that it has dealt with a real-life episode of unemployment (and managed to speak to it even as the phenomenon was still of substantive interest to those experiencing it), and it grounds the explanation of that episode in the extraordinary and perhaps unique shock that so strongly characterizes the period.

At the same time, I can see that the approach has also the defect of its virtues. It is perhaps too easy a game to explain a single episode in a maximally pleasing way without the constraint that the model, enriched with a full menu of shocks, be able to fit booms and other depressions as well. Unfortunately, to look for the same compact explanation of other depressions will prove a vain quest if, as I suppose possible—like Tolstoy's unhappy families—each is depressed in its own way.

## Notes

1. The idea had not been altogether unrecognized, of course. David Hume knew a thing or two about the subject. But classical theory, from Smith to Samuelson and Debreu and beyond, cannot incorporate it and remain classical.  ⸱

2. Mention might be made in this connection of the work by Malinvaud (1980) and by Kouri (1979, 1982) on the effect of the real-supply price of labour upon profitability and growth of the capital stock and of market share. At this point, however, I am concerned with how it

could happen that the real-demand price has fallen below the real-supply price, leaving the latter too high.

## References

Bean, Christopher, Layard, Richard, and Nickell, Steven (1986) 'The Rise in Unemployment', *Economica*, 53, Supplement, S1–S23.

Blanchard, Olivier J., and Summers, Lawrence H. (1986a) 'Hysterisis in Unemployment', *European Economic Review*, 30.

—— (1986b) 'Hysterisis and the European Unemployment Problem', *NBER Macroeconomics Annual* 1, Cambridge, Mass.: National Bureau of Economic Research, 15–78.

Bowles, Samuel (1979) 'A Marxian Model of Unemployment', Lecture, Columbia University.

Bruno, Michael D., and Sachs, Jeffrey, D. (1985) *Economics of Worldwide Stagflation*, Cambridge, Mass.: Harvard University Press.

Calvo, Guillermo (1979) 'Quasi-Walrasian Models of Unemployment', *American Economic Review*, 69 (May) 102–7.

Drazen, Allan and Gottfries, Nils (1987) 'Seniority Rulkes and the Persistence of Unemployment in a Dynamic Optimizing Model', Institute for International Economic Studies, University of Stockholm (Aug.).

Fellner, William J. (1959) 'Demand Inflation, Cost Inflation, and Collective Bargaining', in Phillip D. Bradley, ed., *The Public Stake in Union Power*, Charlottesville: University of Virginia Press.

Fitoussi, Jean-Paul, and Phelps, Edmund S. (1988) *The Slump in Europe*, Oxford: Blackwell.

Gottfries, Nils, and Horn, Hendrik (1987) 'Wage Formation and the Persistence of Unemployment', *Economic Journal*, 97 (Dec.).

Hall, Robert E. (1970) 'Unionism and the Inflationary Bias of Labor Markets', University of California, Berkeley, mimeo. (Jan.).

Hicks, John (1973) *The Crisis in Keynesian Economics*, Oxford: Blackwell.

Lindbeck, Assar, and Snower, Dennis J. (1989) *Unemployment and Wages: The Insider–Outsider Approach*, Cambridge, Mass.: MIT Press.

Kouri, Pentti J. K. (1979) 'Profitability and Growth in a Small Open Economy', in A. Lindbeck, ed., *Inflation and Employment in Open Economies*, Amsterdam: North-Holland.

—— (1982) 'Profitability and Growth', *Scandinavian Journal of Economics*, 84 (June), 317–39.

McDonald, Ian M., and Solow, Robert M. (1981) 'Wage Bargaining and Employment', *American Economic Review*, 71 (Dec.), 896–908.

Malinvaud, Edmond (1980) *Profitability and Unemployment*, Cambridge: Cambridge University Press.

Oswald, Andrew J. (1985) 'The Economic Theory of Trade Unions: An Introductory Survey', *Scandinavian Journal of Economics*, 87, Supplement, 160–93.

—— (1988) 'Unions and Unemployment: Introduction', *European Economic Review*, 32, 695–7.

Phelps, Edmund S. (1968) 'Money–Wage Dynamics and Labor-Market Equilibrium', *Journal of Political Economy*, 76/4, Part 2 (Aug.), 678–711.

—— (1972) *Inflation Policy and Unemployment Theory*, New York: W. W. Norton.

—— (1988a) 'A Working Model of Slump and Recovery from Disturbances to Capital-Goods Demand in an Open Nonmonetary Economy', *American Economic Review, Papers and Proceedings*, 78 (May), 346–50.

—— (1988b) 'A Working Model of Slump and Recovery from Disturbances to Capital-Goods Demand in a Closed Non-monetary Economy', International Monetary Fund, Research Department, Working Paper 88/82 (Aug.); forthcoming, E. J. Nell and W. Semmler, eds., *Nicholas Kaldor and Mainstream Economics*, London: Macmillan.

—— (1988c) ' "Aggregate Demand" in a Non-Monetary Model of Labor-Market and Product-Market Equilibrium', Columbia University, mimeo. (Nov.).

—— (1989, forthcoming) 'An Extended Working Model of Slump and Recovery from Disturbances to Capital-Goods Prices in an Overlapping-Generations Closed Economy: "IS-LM" without Money', in Carsten Heyn-Johnson, ed., *IS-LM after Fifty Years*, London: Macmillan.

Salop, Steven C. (1979) 'A Model of the Natural Rate of Unemployment', *American Economic Review*, 69 (Mar.), 117–25.

Solow, Robert M. (1986) 'Getting the Questions Right', *Economica*, 53, Supplement, S23–S35.

Stiglitz, Joseph E. (1974) 'Wage Determination and Unemployment in LDCs', *Quarterly Journal of Economics*, 88 (May), 194–227.

—— (1986) 'Theories of Wage Rigidity', in J. Butkiewicz, ed., *Keynes' Economic Legacy*, New York: Praeger.

# Index

Kydland, Finn E. 37, 83

Laffer, Arthur B. 79
Lal, Deepak 77
Layard, Richard 98
Leijonhufvud, Axel 8, 17
LeRoy, Steven 8
Lindbeck, Assar 95, 101
Lipsey, Richard G. 58
Long, John 83
Lucas, Jr., Robert E. 31, 42, 46, 85, 87
 and Lucas 'critique' 31–2
 and Lucas supply curve 46–7

McDonald, Ian M. 98
McKean, Roland 67
Malinvaud, Edmond 105
Mankiw, N. Gregory 6, 34, 47, 61
Mayer, Colin 6
Meade, James E. 68, 78, 79
Metzler, Lloyd 44
'menu' costs 57, 61–2
Modigliani, Franco 34, 68
Mors, Matthias 6
Mortensen, Dale 58
Mundell, Robert A. 67, 69, 70, 71
 and policy mix 69–72
Muth, John 42, 43

natural rate of unemployment 14, 33, 94–6, 97–8, 99–100
 *see also* 'incentive-wage' theory
neo-neoclassical theory 83
Nerlove, Marc 43
Nickell, Steven 98

O'Flaherty, Brendan 1
oil shocks 23, 24
Okun, Arthur M. 61, 63
Oswald, Andrew 63, 101

Parkin, Michael 46, 52, 63
Patinkin, Don 44
Pazos, Felipe 56
Pemberton, James 7
Penati, Alessandro 86
persistence 47,–8
Phelps, Edmund 6, 7, 12, 34, 37, 38, 48, 52, 53, 68, 78, 79, 86, 95, 101–3, 104
 and shocks to real interest rate and natural unemployment 102–5

and 'wage-wage' labour-market theory 12–14, 23, 43–4
Phillips, A. W. 12, 35, 43
Pigou, Arthur Cecil 79
Plosser, Charles 83
policy mix 67–8, 73
 neo-Keynesian 68–9
 supply-side 69–75
Prescott, Edward C. 34, 83

Ramsey, Frank P. 34, 79, 91
Rappaport, Bruce 47
Rapping, Leonard A. 85, 87
rational expectations 19–21, 39, 42, 45–6
real wage rigidity 97
real wage stickiness 99
Rebelo, Sergio 83
Roberts, John 23
Rodriguez, Carlos 67, 73
Romer, Cristina 36
Romer, David 47

Sachs, Jeffrey D. 101
Sadka, Eugene 79
Salop, Steven C. 95
Samuelson, Paul 42, 44, 68, 69
Sargent, Thomas J. 42, 48
Shapiro, Matthew 36
Sheshinsky, Eytan 61
Sims, Christopher 31
single agent 83
Sinn, Hans Werner 77
Snower, Dennis J. 95, 101
Solow, Robert M. 98
speculation 6–7
staggering of nominal commitments 48, 52–4, 60–1, 62–3
Stiglitz, Joseph E. 95, 98
Summers, Lawrence H. 6, 101

Taylor, John B. 53, 54, 60
Tobin, James 8, 12, 18, 68
 Tobin's 'q' 8, 9–11, 15–17, 26, 29

van Wijnbergen, Sweder 77
Velupillai, Kumaraswamy 68, 78, 79
Vines, David 68, 78
Wadhwani, S. B. 6
war, prospect of 15–16
Weiss, Yoram 61
Winter, Sidney G. 104

Yellen, Janet 61